I have long believed that it is the duty of Christian leadership to teach truth and expose error. Dr. Walston does this in this book. He alleviates confusion and wrong perceptions about speaking in tongues.

—*Dr. Randy Weiss,*
Director of Crosstalk Television Ministries

Rick Walston challenges long held interpretations of classical Pentecostalism that tongues are the initial physical evidence of Spirit baptism. He is also challenging and changing Pentecostal minds.

—*Tyler S. Ramey, Ph.D. Candidate,*
Director of Truth Enterprises

Dr. Walston points out in a scholarly manner that Luke mentions tongues speaking in only three instances. He shows exegetically and deductively that Luke stresses the salvation rather than the charismatic aspects of those experiences.

—*Dr. Jack Hunka, Pentecostal Assemblies of Canada*
minister, and president of Biblical Seminaries Ukraine

The Speaking in Tongues Controversy

The Initial, Physical Evidence of the Baptism in the Holy Spirit Debate

Rick Walston

Wipf & Stock
PUBLISHERS
Eugene, Oregon

Wipf and Stock Publishers
199 W 8th Ave, Suite 3
Eugene, OR 97401

The Speaking in Tongues Controversy
The Initial, Physical Evidence of the Baptism in the Holy Spirit Debate
By Walston, Rick
Copyright©2003 by Walston, Rick
ISBN: 1-59752-165-5
Publication date 5/2/2005
Previously published by Xulon Press, 2003

Unless otherwise indicated, Bible quotations are taken from the Holy Bible International Version. Copyright © 1973, 1978, 1984 by The International Bible Society. Used by permission of Zondervan Bible Publishers.

Table of Contents

Chapter 1
    Background Information 11

Chapter 2
    Do All Speak in Tongues? 19

Chapter 3
    The Initial, Physical Evidence of the Baptism
    in the Holy Spirit 25

Chapter 4
    Straw Men and Authorial Intent 43

Chapter 5
    Argument # 1: Authorial Intent 59

Chapter 6
    Argument # 2: Three Times out of Five?
    Does this Establish a Paradigm? 113

Chapter 7
    Argument # 3: The Age to Come 129

Chapter 8
    Argument # 4: Subsequence 141

Chapter 9
    Argument # 5:
    Historical Narrative versus Didactic 145

Chapter 10
    History: Not on the Side of Evidence 155

Chapter 11
　　Why Tongues? 163

Chapter 12
　　Are Tongues the Least? 171

Chapter 13
　　Evidence or Accompaniment? 183

Chapter 14
　　A Recapitulation and Concluding Remarks 191

Chapter 15
　　Study Questions 203

Bibliography 223

Glossary 231

About the Author 235

Chapter 1

Background Information

While writing this book, I had input from various sources. Since it is specifically about a topic that is near and dear to Pentecostals, I especially wanted feedback from some of my colleagues. I was a bit taken aback by the passion which greeted me from those who reviewed the early manuscript, and it was from those responses that the title of this book emerged. Pentecostals from both sides of this debate were equally emotional. Some thought that this book would be just the right thing to help others understand the truth, and a few thought otherwise. Some lauded my "biblical stand," while others implied that I had apparently suffered a mind-altering blow to the head.

My Personal Background

First, it should be understood that while I have a varied and eclectic background in both education and practical ministry, I most identify with the movement known as Trinitarian Pentecostalism. I cannot say that I started out my Christian life in 1975 as a Pentecostal, but I was soon attracted to the theology (which I felt was more consistent with a loving God who intervenes in the lives of his children) and the passion found in Pentecostal circles. I had always had a disdain for the "dead and dry" (in whatever area of life), and I was inexorably drawn to fellowship with Pentecostal believers. However, not only do I have a disdain for the "dead and dry," I also have always had disdain for the obtuse and gullible. So, almost as soon as I became a Christian in 1975, I enrolled in formal college-level Bible and theology studies. Since then, I have been a student of the Christian faith.

However, after all these years, I still identify with Trinitarian Pentecostalism. I still find myself drawn to both the theology and passion of my Pentecostal roots. Thus, I do not write on this subject as an outsider, as one reviewer suggested.

Of "Norm," "Normative," and "Normal"

For many years (20 in fact) I held the traditional position of the Classical Pentecostals. While pastoring in Assemblies of God churches and later in independent churches, I continued to hold and teach the Classical Pentecostal position that speaking in tongues was (is) the initial, physical evidence of the baptism in the Holy Spirit, and that it was a "norm" for all Christians.

The words "norm" and "normative" in this book (and most generally in theological language) mean something that is a "must." It is a "have to." For example, it is a "norm" (or "normative") that people be born-again to be saved. Some may not call it being "born-again," but the reality of the spiritual experience is the same.[1] So, "norm" (and "normative") means "have to" not "may" or "might." A "norm" (or "normative") is something that is *incumbent upon all Christians for all time.*

There should be a broad distinction between something being a "norm" (or "normative") and something being "normal" and repeatable. For example, it is *normal* that some Christians be called to be missionaries, but it is not a "norm" (a "have to") for all Christians to be called as missionaries. Maybe this table will help clarify:

Norm & Normative	**Normal (repeatable)**
Have to happen	May happen
Shall be every time	Is occasional as God directs

The two basic positions, then, go like this. (1) The Baptism in the Holy Spirit always leads to speaking in tongues as a "norm" for all believers. (2) The Baptism in the Holy Spirit may lead to speaking in tongues for some believers as a "normal" spiritual experience.

Gordon Fee explains the use of these terms this way:

> I have tried to explicate carefully . . . "norm" and "normative" have to do with "must" and "have to," not with "may" or the "valid repetition" of what was assumed as "normal" for them. Jesus does not establish a norm that we would pluck grain on the Sabbath;

> rather he illustrates that Sabbath was made for humans not humans for the Sabbath. That Sabbath was made for humans I would indeed consider as normative, but not that one must pluck grain to demonstrate it to be so.[2]

The Classical Pentecostal position is that it is not just "normal" that Christians speak in tongues as the evidence of the baptism in the Holy Spirit, but that it is the "norm" (a have-to). Thus, for them, if a Christian does not speak in tongues, it means the person has not received the baptism in the Holy Spirit. And this is the position that I held for many years.

My Shift

In 1995, I was teaching an adult Sunday school class at the church I pastored. In that class was a man named Tom Hight. I was teaching hermeneutics, and at some point in the class I was discussing the various genres of Scripture and didactic versus historical narrative and how we are to exegete them based upon their own inherent principles. It was then that Tom asked me a pointed question about how my hermeneutics played out in my theological understanding that speaking in tongues was the initial, physical evidence of the baptism in the Holy Spirit. From my previous statements on these hermeneutical principles, and from the way he worded his question, I was left speechless. I scratched my head and replied that I would have to get back to him with my answer. This was the impetus that sent me researching a position that I had long held almost by default.

After a few of months of research and study of the Scriptures, I addressed my Sunday school class and announced that Tom's pointed question had sent me on a life-changing journey. I had changed my position on the issue of tongues as evidence. Still a Pentecostal and still the senior pastor of the church, I had shifted to what I consider to be a more biblical position. It would take several years before I could articulate my position, and some may think that I have several more years to go.

This book opens up to you my research on this topic. It shows what for me were significant arguments that convinced me that speaking in tongues is *not* the initial, physical evidence of the baptism in the Holy Spirit.

Speaking in Tongues is Normal for Today

With that said, I would like to make this very important point: While I no longer believe that speaking in tongues is a *norm*, I do believe that it is *a normal* Christian experience. I still believe that speaking in tongues is a valuable aspect of my personal devotional life, and it is a valuable part of the spiritual lives of millions of Bible-believing Christians. Speaking in tongues is a good gift from God, and it is both operational and desirable today.

Pentecostals as a whole try very hard to allow the Scriptures to establish their creeds and practices. Over the years, I have been both humored and dismayed by the caricatures painted of Pentecostals that make us appear as though we willy-nilly place all experiences above Scripture. This is far from the truth. Throughout my time as a student and teacher in Pentecostal circles, I always heard—with consistent regularity—that the Bible is our *sole rule of faith and practice*. The constant refrain from leader and layman alike is a well-worn quotation of Paul:

> All Scripture is God-breathed and is useful for teaching, rebuking, correcting and training in righteousness, so that the man of God may be thoroughly equipped for every good work (2 Tim. 3:16-17).

Others may disagree with the Pentecostal understanding or interpretation of the Bible. This is acceptable. But to teach that Pentecostals *simply place their experiences above the Scripture* is neither accurate nor benign. So, let it be established that Pentecostals are not in any way attempting to argue that their experiences have precedence over Scripture. They are simply arguing that their experiences are reflected in the Scriptures.

My goal in this book is to show why I disagree with the traditional Pentecostal interpretation of Scripture on this hotly debated topic of speaking in tongues as the initial, physical evidence of the baptism in the Holy Spirit. It is not my desire to inflame my Pentecostal colleagues. It *is* my desire, however, to look at the biblical evidence together in order to see if the Classical Pentecostal position stands up to the Scriptures that we all hold dear.

End Notes

[1] Verses showing the need to be "born again" include:

> In reply Jesus declared, "I tell you the truth, no one can see the kingdom of God unless he is born again" (John 3:3).

> But when the kindness and love of God our Savior appeared, he saved us, not because of righteous things we had done, but because of his mercy. He saved us through the washing of rebirth and renewal by the Holy Spirit, whom he poured out on us generously through Jesus Christ our Savior, so that, having been justified by his grace, we might become heirs having the hope of eternal life (Titus 3:4-7).

> For you have been born again, not of perishable seed, but of imperishable, through the living and enduring word of God (1 Peter 1:23).

[2] Gordon D. Fee, "Response to Roger Stronstad's 'The Biblical Precedent for Historical Precedent,'" *Paraclete* (Summer 1993), pp. 13-14.

Chapter 2

Do All Speak in Tongues?

Many who do not understand the categorization of speaking in tongues by Classical Pentecostals assume that Paul's rhetorical question, "Do all speak in tongues?" settles the issue. In this passage, Paul explains that we are all members of the body of Christ, and, as such, each of us has a different function. So, not every believer will function in the same gift. In this passage Paul says:

> Now you are the body of Christ, and each one of you is a part of it. And in the church God has appointed first of all apostles, second prophets, third teachers, then workers of miracles, also those having gifts of healing, those able to help others, those with gifts of administration, and those speaking in different kinds of tongues. Are all apostles? Are all prophets? Are all teachers? Do all work miracles? Do all have gifts of healing?

Do all speak in tongues? Do all interpret (1 Corinthians 12:27-30)?

Clearly, not everyone is an apostle, or a prophet, or a teacher. Likewise, not everyone works miracles, has the gift of healing,[1] or speaks in tongues. So, why do the Classical Pentecostals say that all may speak in tongues when they are baptized in the Holy Spirit? Doesn't this Pentecostal position stand in direct opposition to Paul's teaching that not all speak in tongues?

The Complexity of Tongues

The gift of tongues is a complex gift, and it may have more variables of operation and function than any other gift. Briefly, Classical Pentecostals (and many others) see two major categories for speaking in tongues.

First, tongues are seen as a prayer language in the Holy Spirit (Acts 2:4; 1 Corinthians 14:14-17), and according to Classical Pentecostals *in this context* all Christians may speak (pray) in tongues.

Second, speaking in tongues is seen as one of the manifestations of the Spirit of 1 Corinthians 12. And *in this context* not all shall speak in tongues (1 Corinthians 12:30) as Paul clearly implies.

Speaking in tongues can lead to personal edification (1 Corinthians 14:4), but it also functions as a means of edification of the body of Christ (1 Corinthians 12:7, 14:5). It may function as a type of prayer (1 Corinthians 14:15). It may be exercised as a form of worship and praise (1 Corinthians 14:15-16), and in this context the message of the tongues is directed to God not to men (1 Corinthians 14:2).

However, speaking in tongues is also an avenue in which messages are given to man from God (1 Corinthians 14:21) and when interpreted, the message is equal to prophecy in edification (1 Corinthians 14:5). It may even function as a sign of judgment to unbelievers (1 Corinthians 14:22).

Thus, there are many functions of speaking in tongues. Those who hold to only one aspect of this gift miss the biblical variables. For instance, one might argue that tongues cannot be used to edify the body of Christ since Paul said that when one speaks in tongues, he is edifying himself (1 Corinthians 14:4). But, another passage is forgotten. Paul also said that tongues, when interpreted, have the same value to the body of Christ as prophecy, which *is* edifying for the body (1 Corinthians 14:5).

Devotional Tongues and the Gift of Tongues

In Pentecostal theology, there are two essential and major distinctions of the function of speaking in tongues. First, there are what may be called *devotional tongues* or *prayer language*. This *prayer language* is seen throughout the book of Acts as well as in 1 Corinthians. Paul says, "For if I *pray* in a tongue, my spirit prays, but my mind is unfruitful" (1 Corinthians 14:14, emphasis added). Classical Pentecostals believe that all Christians may pray in tongues by virtue of their relationship with the Holy Spirit.[2]

Next, there is that function of tongues which is manifested in the gathered assembly for the purpose of edifying the church when there is the complementary gift of interpretation in operation. This is "messages in tongues" in the gathered assembly. Classical Pentecostals do *not* believe that all Christians shall speak in tongues in this function. Thus, when Paul says that not everyone speaks in tongues, it is the function of the *gift of tongues* found in 1 Corinthians 12:10 (not the *prayer language*) to which he refers.

The table below gives an outline view of some of the scriptural distinctions between tongues as a *prayer language* in the Holy Spirit and the *gift of tongues* as in 1 Corinthians 12:30.

SCRIPTURAL DISTINCTIONS OF TONGUES

As a Gift of Tongues	As a Prayer Language
1 Cor. 12:30	Acts 2:4, 10:24-44, 19:6-7
Not all speak in tongues	All spoke in tongues
1 Cor. 14:27-28	Acts 2:4, 10:24-44, 19:6-7
Must interpret	No interpretation
1 Cor. 14:27	Acts 2:4, 10:24-44, 19:6-7
Two or three to speak	Number not limited
1 Cor. 12:10	Acts 2:4, 10:24-44, 1 Cor. 14:14-17
Gift of tongues in assembly	Tongues as a prayer language

For the most part, it is the general view of Pentecostals that there is a basic essence of similarity between *the gift of tongues* (as a message to the body, 1 Corinthians 12:30) and speaking in tongues as a *prayer language* (Acts 2:4, 10:24-44). They are both speaking in unknown tongues by the power of the Holy Spirit; however, the purpose (or function) of each is different.

They are the same form, but they serve different functions. Thus there is a distinction to be made between the *gift of tongues* and tongues as a *prayer language*.³

These two essential and major distinctions of tongues are why a simple appeal to 1 Corinthians 12:30, "Do all speak in tongues?" does not settle the issue. The Pentecostal agrees wholeheartedly with the apostle Paul on this point: Not everyone will have the *gift of tongues* (as in 1 Corinthians 12:10) and utter messages in the gathered assembly. In fact, not even all those who speak in tongues as a *prayer language* will have the *gift of tongues* (1 Corinthians 12:10) to utter messages in the gathered assembly. Yet, for the Classical Pentecostal, everyone may speak in tongues as a *devotional prayer language*, which (for them) is the attending, initial, physical evidence of the baptism in the Holy Spirit.

End Notes

[1] In the Greek, the manifestation of the Spirit known as the *gifts of healing* is in the plural, and it is properly called the *gifts of healings*. In all three places where this gift is mentioned (1 Corinthians 12, verse 9, 28, and 30), it is consistently used in the plural. I will use it in the singular however as is popularly done.

[2] While I do not support the Classical Pentecostal position that speaking in tongues is the initial, physical evidence of the baptism in the Holy Spirit, I nonetheless

do believe that tongues may function as a prayer (and praise) language, which is not the same as receiving the *gift of tongues* in the assembly.

³ Gordon D. Fee, *God's Empowering Presence: The Holy Spirit in the Letters of Paul.* (Peabody, MA.: Hendrickson Publishers, Inc., 1994), p. 582. While Gordon Fee does not believe that speaking in tongues is the initial, physical evidence of the baptism in the Holy Spirit, he does make the distinction between tongues as a "prayer language" and the "gift of tongues" for the gathered assembly.

Chapter 3

The Initial, Physical Evidence of the Baptism in the Holy Spirit

The Scales of Truth

This book is an argument for a position. It is not unlike a prosecutor attempting to convince a jury that his position is true and his opponent's position is false (or inaccurate). So, you are the jury, and you are about to read my argument.

As humans, we all would like to see a *coup de grâce*. A *coup de grâce* is the *finishing stroke*, or as they often say in court trials, "the smoking gun." Every jury would like to see that undeniable piece of evidence that *proves* that the defendant is guilty because that would make their job easier in making their decision.

The *coup de grâce* might be the murder weapon with the defendant's bloody finger prints on it. It might be a video tape that shows the defendant in the act of committing the crime. It might be several reliable eye witnesses who all agree in their testimony that the defendant was the man who committed the crime. The *finishing stroke* is that one piece of physical evidence that convinces the jury that the defendant is guilty.

However, sometimes, there is no single *coup de grâce*. Sometimes, it is the accumulated, overwhelming circumstantial evidence presented against the defendant that convinces a jury. If the *circumstantial evidence* is weighty enough, it may be convincing to the jury that the defendant is guilty. Circumstantially, the defendant may have had motive, opportunity, and capability. For example, he may have no alibi for the time of the murder. He may have been the only person who wanted the other person dead. He may have been the only person with the means and opportunity to murder the person. People have been found guilty in criminal cases without a shred of physical evidence because the weight of circumstantial evidence was so overwhelming that the jury was convinced that the defendant was guilty.

A *Coup de Grâce* or Circumstantial Evidence

My arguments may supply a *coup de grâce* for some readers. For these people, my comments on a certain verse, a specific argument, or a hermeneutical principle might be the *finishing stroke* which convinces them. Others, however, might not see a clear *coup de grâce* at all.

For those who do not see a clear *finishing stroke*, I ask that you to simply "weigh" the circumstantial evidence of the arguments presented herein. Think of it as a pair of scales. Place the *accumulated argumentation* on one scale and place the *opponent's accumulated argument* on the other scale and see which one weighs more. Once you have seriously considered the arguments in this book, then make your decision as to which position tips the scales in its favor.

Opening Statement

For many years Classical Pentecostal scholars have taught that speaking in tongues, i.e., in the prayer language, is the *initial, physical* evidence of the baptism in the Holy Spirit.[1] However, is there biblical evidence to warrant this Classical Pentecostal position?

This book argues that the *tongues-as-evidence position* cannot be biblically supported. In fact, I shall show that the main book, i.e., Acts—from which this Classical Pentecostal peculiarity is derived—does not teach this idea at all. I will advance five arguments in this book. Each argument opposes the position that speaking in tongues is the initial, physical evidence of the baptism in the Holy Spirit. After the five arguments, other supporting data will be given.

Authorial Intent in the Book of Acts

(1) The first and most powerful argument for me is *authorial intent*. In chapter five, I establish that Luke clearly conveyed a predominantly soteriological (salvation) and not pneumatological (spiritual gifts) theme throughout the book of Acts. I walk the reader through every passage in Acts that contains the germane phrases to the issue such as "speaking in tongues," "filled with the

Holy Spirit," and "baptized in the Holy Spirit." While this is not a commentary on the book of Acts, it is a definitive representation of Luke's comments throughout Acts on this particular topic.

Deductive Reasoning

(2) Next, in chapter six, I take a look at inductive and deductive reasoning with reference to the number of biblical examples of speaking in tongues. While Classical Pentecostals claim that there are three explicit references to speaking in tongues out of five Holy-Spirit baptism accounts, I show that there are three out of twenty-six.

Citizenship in the Age to Come

(3) The third argument, in chapter seven, is based on *citizenship in the age to come*. It shows that unless a person is filled with the Spirit, he is not a Christian at all. This position is that to be saved is to be filled with the Spirit. Thus, all Christians are filled with (i.e., baptized in) the Spirit, but not all who are filled with the Holy Spirit speak in tongues.

Argument of Subsequence

(4) Next, in chapter eight, I address the argument of subsequence. I show that the sequence of events for salvation/Spirit baptism/speaking in tongues is not consistent; thus, no one way is normative. (The word "normative" is used here in the same sense as "norm," in that it is incumbent upon all Christians at all times in all places.)

Historical Narrative versus Didactic

(5) In chapter nine I touch on the historical narrative versus didactic argument. This argument sets out the proposition that our doctrines (normative theology) must be based predominantly on didactic portions of Scripture, not narrative ones.

A Background on Pentecostalism and the Divisions within the Groups

It is important to make a few points of clarification. There are some basic terms that are often misunderstood and misapplied. In the church, there have historically been "Three Pentecostal Waves."

The First Wave	*The Second Wave*	*The Third Wave*
1901 to present	*1950's to present*	*1980's to present*
Classical Pentecostals & Pentecostals	Charismatics	Signs & Wonders

The First Wave

The first wave (or "movement") is Classical Pentecostalism. It is thought to have begun in 1901 when Agnes Ozman spoke in tongues at the the school that Charles Fox Parham had begun, Bethel Bible School in Topeka, Kansas. A *Classical Pentecostal* is one who believes these three primary things about the *baptism in the Holy Spirit:*

(a) The baptism in the Holy Spirit is a second work of grace that happens sometime after conversion. In some cases, this baptism may happen so immediately after salvation—as in the case of the Cornelius household, see Acts 10—that the first work (salvation) and the second work of the infilling of the Holy Spirit can appear (or are) simultaneous.

(b) The baptism in the Holy Spirit will be initially evidenced by speaking tongues. Speaking in tongues, then, for the Classical Pentecostal, is the *initial, physical* evidence of this baptism.

(c) The evidence of speaking in tongues is a norm for all Christians. Thus, all Christians who are baptized in the Holy Spirit *shall* speak in tongues.

However, there have been false and misleading charges for years saying that Classical Pentecostals teach that people must speak in tongues to be saved. This is simply not true. I know of no truly Classical Pentecostal denomination or fellowship that teaches this false idea.[2]

Some attempt to arrive at this conclusion by saying that though Classical Pentecostals do not explicitly teach that one must speak in tongues to be saved, this is still the outcome of their theology. The argument says that since Classical Pentecostals teach that speaking in tongues is the evidence of the infilling of the Holy Spirit, if one does not speak in tongues then one is not filled with the Holy Spirit. And a person without the Holy Spirit is not a Christian. However, those who make this argument misunderstand Classical Pentecostal theology on the issue of Holy-Spirit baptism. While it shall be dealt with more later, suffice it to say that Classical Pentecostals teach that all Christians "have" the Holy Spirit at conversion. Thus, one does not have to speak in tongues to have the

Holy Spirit and to be "baptized *by* the Holy Spirit into the body of Christ" (1 Corinthians 12:13). The "baptism *in* the Holy Spirit" with the evidence of speaking in tongues is not the initiation of the Holy Spirit into a believer's life; for them it is a spiritual experience subsequent to a person's conversion experience.[3] Even the Classical Pentecostals' construct of their position states that the baptism in the Holy Spirit with the evidence of speaking in tongues happens post conversion. So, obviously, before one speaks in tongues, one is already saved.

Subdivided

Within the first "wave," there is a distinction that some make which I think is helpful. This distinction is between the terms *Classical Pentecostal* and simply *Pentecostal*. One may be a First Wave Pentecostal without being a First Wave *Classical* Pentecostal. And though I do use these terms (*Classical Pentecostal* and *Pentecostal*) interchangeably in this work, technically these two terms are not synonymous. A First Wave Pentecostal is to be distinguished from a First Wave Classical Pentecostal in that the Pentecostal, while believing in the continuation of all the gifts, does not agree with his Classical Pentecostal brothers and sisters that speaking in tongues is the *initial, physical evidence* of the baptism in the Holy Spirit nor that all Christians who are baptized in the Holy Spirit shall speak in tongues. Yet, the Classical Pentecostal and the Pentecostal both come from the same church background, generally known as the holiness movements.[4] This then leads to yet another title that must be identified and distinguished, that of charismatic.

The Second Wave

The "second wave" is the "charismatic renewal movement" or charismatics.[5] In the 1950s and 1960s, some people in mainline denominations (e.g., Episcopal, Lutheran, Presbyterian, Roman Catholic, and Greek Orthodox) started experiencing the supernatural gifts of the Spirit in their midst. These charismatics accepted the continuation of the gifts of the Spirit, but (like the Pentecostals) they rejected the Classical Pentecostal teaching that speaking in tongues was the *initial, physical evidence* of the baptism in the Holy Spirit.

So, a charismatic is a person who (a) believes in the perpetuity of spiritual gifts but (b) does not believe that speaking in tongues is the *initial, physical evidence* of the baptism in the Holy Spirit, and (c) who comes from (historically speaking) mainline churches/denominations.

So, while the Classical Pentecostals and the Pentecostals have their church history in common, the charismatics and the Pentecostals have their theology in common, at least on the issue of tongues as evidence.

The Third Wave

More recently, in the 1980's, there came a movement called the "Third Wave" or the "Signs and Wonders" movement. Many evangelicals who do not consider themselves charismatics, Pentecostals, or Classical Pentecostals, yet accept the perpetuity of the gifts have been attracted to this new group. Third Wavers believe that the Baptism in the Holy Spirit happens at conversion, and speaking in tongues in not considered the initial, physical evidence thereof. A couple of names identified with the Third Wave are C. Peter Wagner and John Wimber, the founder of the Vineyard Christian Church.

The Pros and Cons

It is sad that a quick Internet search of these three "waves" brings up some of the most ridiculous misinformation available. While all three waves have had their problems, the same can be said for every denomination and theological camp. So, yes, there have been problematic issues within these "waves," but people should be careful not to over generalize. For example, *The United Pentecostal Church* with its aberrant teachings should not be lumped together with Classical Pentecostals, and the "Third Wave" does not have its roots in the occult. It is amazing to me how much damaging propaganda can be disseminated by misinformed people, or, even worse, disingenuous people with an agenda.

My Use of the Terms

From this point on I shall use the terms *Classical Pentecostal* and *Pentecostal* to refer to the historical Classical Pentecostals. Thus, I use them interchangeably in this work for the sake of ease and to limit the repetitive use of the term Classical Pentecostal. (In spite of this interchange of the two terms, it should be remembered that a person can be considered a Pentecostal without being a Classical Pentecostal.)

The Pentecostal World Fellowship

One area of misunderstanding, especially among those outside the Pentecostal camps, is the idea that most Pentecostals no longer believe that speaking in tongues is the initial, physical evidence of the baptism in the Holy Spirit. This is simply not true. Perhaps part of the reason for this misunderstanding is the over generalization of the three waves into one collective whole. I have spoken with non-Pentecostal churchmen who seem to think that anyone who believes that the gifts are for today is a Pentecostal. Thus, when they speak to a charismatic, to a third waver, or to a first wave Pentecostal, they might get the idea that Pentecostals no longer believe that speaking in tongues is the initial, physical evidence of the baptism in the Holy Spirit. However, there are many Pentecostals who do: they are called *Classical Pentecostals*, and that theological distinction is what gives them their title.

While there are, and always have been, first wave Pentecostals who do not hold to this particular idea, the majority of first wave Pentecostals do. In fact, the largest group of Pentecostals is called the Pentecostal World Fellowship (PWF), which was organized in 1947. The PWF meets triennially in major cities around the world, including Zurich (1947), Paris (1949), London (1952), Toronto (1958), Jerusalem (1961), Helsinki (1964), Rio de Janeiro (1967), Dallas, Texas (1970), Seoul (1973), London (1976), Vancouver, British Columbia (1979), Nairobi (1982), Zurich (1985), Singapore (1989), Oslo (1992), Jerusalem (1995), Seoul, Korea (1998), Los Angeles (2001), and Johannesburg, South Africa (2004).

The PWF Statement of Faith is thoroughly orthodox, conservative, and evangelical. In fact, most Christian churches would fully agree with their tenets, except this particular one:

> We Believe: in the baptism of the Holy Spirit with the evidence of speaking in other tongues as the Spirit gives the utterance according to Acts 2:4, and in the operation of the spiritual gifts and ministries.

Since there is no larger organization that represents more Christian Pentecostals than the PWF, and since their statement of faith is a reflection of their constituents, it is safe to say that the majority of First Wave Pentecostals continue to believe that speaking in tongues is the *initial, physical* evidence of the baptism in the Holy Spirit.

Initial and Physical

Also, it should be noted that for the Classical Pentecostal, the words *initial* and *physical* modify the word evidence. Non-Pentecostals often forget or do not know this aspect of Classical Pentecostal theology. Thus, *initial* means first, and *physical* means outward. Pentecostals do not deny that there are other, later, evidences of the baptism in the Holy Spirit, like, for example, the ability to be Christ's witnesses: "But you will receive power when the Holy Spirit comes on you; and you will be my witnesses in Jerusalem, and in all Judea and Samaria, and to the ends of the earth" (Acts 1:8), or the fruit of the Spirit: "But the fruit of the Spirit is love, joy, peace, patience, kindness, goodness, faithfulness, gentleness and self-control" (Galatians 5:22-23a). Thus, it should be kept in mind that Classical Pentecostals do *not* teach that speaking in tongues is simply "the evidence of the baptism in the Holy Spirit"; they teach that speaking in tongues is the *initial, physical* evidence of the baptism in the Holy Spirit.

The Term "Baptized in the Holy Spirit"

Pentecostals make much of the term "baptized (or baptism) in the Holy Spirit." The Bible speaks of this *Spirit baptism*, and it clearly depicts Jesus himself as the one who does this baptizing. John the Baptist identifies Jesus as the one who shall baptize people in the Holy Spirit. All four Gospels record John's words about this Spirit baptism:

Matthew 3:11

> I [John the Baptist] baptize you with water for repentance. But after me will come one who is more powerful than I, whose sandals I am not fit to carry. He will baptize you with the Holy Spirit and with fire.[6]

Mark 1:8

> I [John the Baptist] baptize you with water, but he [Jesus Christ] will baptize you with the Holy Spirit.

Luke 3:16

> John [the Baptist] answered them all, "I

baptize you with water. But one more powerful than I will come, the thongs of whose sandals I am not worthy to untie. He [Jesus Christ] will baptize you with the Holy Spirit and with fire."

John 1:33-34

I [John the Baptist] would not have known him, except that the one who sent me to baptize with water told me, "The man on whom you see the Spirit come down and remain is he who will baptize with the Holy Spirit." I have seen and I testify that this is the Son of God.

Water Baptism is not Spirit Baptism

Next, there is a distinction to be made between being baptized in water and being baptized in the Holy Spirit. These are two separate experiences. Nonetheless, some Christians within more liturgical Christian traditions have taught that the Spirit comes to a believer through water baptism. Some have used Jesus' water baptism and the Holy Spirit descending on him as a dove as their paradigm for this position. However, the verses immediately above indicate that Jesus is the one who baptizes in the Holy Spirit. And note that during his earthly sojourn, he never baptized any person in water: "The Pharisees heard that Jesus was gaining and baptizing more disciples than John, although in fact it was not Jesus who baptized, but his disciples" (John 4:1-2).

Furthermore, the fact that water baptism and Spirit baptism are not the same thing is also clearly evidenced in

Acts 10 where Cornelius and his household received the baptism in the Holy Spirit *as Peter preached to them* (Acts 10:44-46). Only after they had already received the baptism in the Holy Spirit did Peter then baptize them in water. Gordon Fee makes this powerful statement: "The result, therefore, is that in no text does Paul associate the gift of the Spirit with water baptism, either as a cause or as occurring experientially at the same time."[7]

Spirit Baptism is the Gift of the Spirit

So, while there is a distinction to be made between being *baptized in water* and being *baptized in the Holy Spirit*, Classical Pentecostals attempt to go further and make a distinction between the initial salvation (conversion) experience and the baptism in the Holy Spirit. Classical Pentecostals argue that there is a difference between receiving the *gift of the Holy Spirit* (also called the *promise of the Father*, Acts 1:4; 2:38) at conversion and receiving the *baptism in the Holy Spirit* (which for them is subsequent to conversion). The baptism in the Holy Spirit is seen as a secondary and subsequent work of grace. In Acts 2, Peter says:

> Repent and be baptized, every one of you, in the name of Jesus Christ for the forgiveness of your sins. And you will receive the gift of the Holy Spirit. The promise is for you and your children and for all who are far off—for all whom the Lord our God will call (Acts 2:38-39).

Classical Pentecostals do not deny that one receives the

"gift of the Holy Spirit" at conversion. They do, however, believe that the "baptism in the Holy Spirit" is something distinct from this "gift of the Holy Spirit" or "promise of the Father." It is to them a fuller relational experience with the Holy Spirit which occurs after conversion (i.e., after one has received the "gift of the Holy Spirit" or "promise of the Father"). However, it is my contention that the Scripture does not make such a distinction. The *promise of the Father* (or the *gift of the Holy Spirit*), which Pentecostals agree is received at conversion, is the same thing as the *baptism in the Holy Spirit*. This is clearly seen in the contexts where the term *promise of the Father* is used.

In Acts 1:4, Jesus tells his disciples that they must wait for "the gift my Father promised." Then, in verse five, he identifies this "promised gift of the Father" as being "baptized with the Holy Spirit."

Acts 1:3-5
> After his suffering, he showed himself to these men and gave many convincing proofs that he was alive. He appeared to them over a period of forty days and spoke about the kingdom of God. On one occasion, while he was eating with them, he gave them this command: "Do not leave Jerusalem, but wait for *the gift my Father promised*, which you have heard me speak about. For John baptized with water, but in a few days you will be *baptized with the Holy Spirit*" (emphasis added).

It is clear that Jesus uses these two phrases to describe one event. Later, Peter likewise uses the phrase "baptized with the Holy Spirit," and he also links it to the "gift of the Holy Spirit."

Acts 11:15-17

> As I began to speak, the Holy Spirit came on them as he had come on us at the beginning. Then I remembered what the Lord had said: "John baptized with water, but you will be *baptized with the Holy Spirit.*" So if *God gave them the same gift* as he gave us, who believed in the Lord Jesus Christ, who was I to think that I could oppose God?

Furthermore, on the day of Pentecost after the disciples had received the baptism in the Holy Spirit, Peter explains to the Jews that they can receive this same experience. "Peter replied, 'Repent and be baptized, every one of you, in the name of Jesus Christ for the forgiveness of your sins. And you will receive the gift of the Holy Spirit'" (Acts 2:38). It is clear from the context that Peter refers to the *baptism in the Holy Spirit* (that which the Jews had observed and were now asking about, Acts 2:12) as the "gift of the Holy Spirit." The *baptism in the Holy Spirit* is the same as the "gift of the Holy Spirit" (Acts 2:38) and as the "promise of the Father" (Acts 1:4). Context will not allow a different interpretation. So, though this topic will be dealt with below for further clarification, it is important to realize at the outset that these terms are used interchangeably throughout the New Testament and shall likewise be used in this fashion throughout this book.

End Notes

[1] It should be clarified that when Classical Pentecostals refer to this "evidence," they are referring to the prayer language of tongues and not to the gift of *messages in tongues* in 1 Corinthians 12. No Classical Pentecostal argues that the initial, physical evidence of the baptism in the Holy Spirit is the gift to utter *messages in tongues* in the gathered assembly. This difference between these two functions of tongues is important to understand; it is the *prayer language* to which the Classical Pentecostal refers when he speaks of the "evidence" of the baptism in the Holy Spirit.

[2] There are two important points that must be noted here: (1) While I know of no Classical Pentecostal *denomination* or *fellowship* that teaches that one must speak in tongues to be saved, I have heard of a few misguided and uninformed Classical Pentecostal individuals who have said such erroneous things. However, to ascribe to a movement the errors of a few within the movement is simply guilt by association. Misinformation and *laymen errors* occur in every denomination and fellowship, but we do not ascribe to the whole the irresponsible comments of a few ignorant or misguided members. (2) It is important also to note that the group of so-called Pentecostals that do teach this aberrant idea is *The United Pentecostal Church*—aka, Jesus Only and Oneness Pentecostals. However, *The United Pentecostal Church* is not a Christian Trinitarian church, and it should not be categorized together with orthodox, Trinitarian, Classical Pentecostals.

[3] For more discussion on this, see chapter seven of

this book.

[4] I was a Classical Pentecostal for about 20 years, but my biblical research into the topic of this book caused me to change my perspective, and today I am simply a First Wave Pentecostal.

[5] More recently in popular Christian parlance, the term "charismatic" has come to be nearly synonymous with the term Pentecostal. While these terms are often, mistakenly, used synonymously, it is important for our study to know the historical differences.

[6] All Scripture quotations are from the New International Version of the Bible unless otherwise noted.

[7] Gordon D. Fee, *God's Empowering Presence: The Holy Spirit in the Letters of Paul* (Peabody, MA.: Hendrickson Publishers, Inc., 1994), p. 862.

Chapter 4

Straw Men and Authorial Intent

Setting the Stage

I am indebted to one Pentecostal colleague who read this manuscript while it was still in its early stages. He chided me for what he perceived to be the logical fallacy of building a "straw man." He said, in essence:

> I think that a significant portion of your argument is a "straw man" argument. You ask, *"Why does Luke not make a point of saying that they did (or did not) speak in tongues?"* [This quote is found in the next chapter.] This supposes that tongues-as-evidence proponents have missed Luke's soteriological intent in the book of Acts and rather insists that his intent is to develop the doctrine of the initial, physical evidence of the baptism in the Holy Spirit. Then, of course, you provide evidence in support of

Luke's intent supposing that this is defeating to the opposing point of view.

A "straw man" argument is an anathema to all who believe in fair play. I was a tongues-as-evidence proponent for many years, and I now honestly attempt to accurately represent their position. After all, it is not a "straw man" position that I disagree with. I disagree with the idea that speaking in tongues is the initial, physical evidence of the baptism in the Holy Spirit, and that it is a norm for all Christians. Thus, I have no need for a "straw man."

I do not believe—nor have I implied—that the tongues-as-evidence proponents have missed Luke's soteriological intent. This would be a charge that would be unfounded. I have been a Pentecostal for nearly 30 years. In that time I pastored in Assemblies of God churches and independent Pentecostal churches. Also, during those years, I have heard many Pentecostal preachers use the book of Acts for salvation messages. So, I am certainly not implying that somehow tongues-as-evidence proponents *miss* the fact that Luke intends to show that people got saved throughout the book of Acts.

However, within the Classical Pentecostal context of the doctrine of initial evidence, I certainly do believe that we Pentecostals have only minored on Lukan soteriology. That is precisely my point. I believe that Classical Pentecostals have *minored on* what Luke *majored on*. Therein lies the problem as I see it, and one that I had to come to terms with in my own theology.

Furthermore, I do not believe that *my premise*

insists that they believe that Luke's intent was to develop the doctrine of the initial, physical evidence of the baptism in the Holy Spirit. It seems apparent that they themselves implicitly (sometimes explicitly) insist such by their arguments.

Actually, I am *surprised* that I have to establish that tongues-as-evidence proponents emphasize the pneumatological (i.e., charismatic, not soteriological) nature of the book of Acts. I honestly thought that such a fact was not in question by tongues-as-evidence proponents or by others. Most people (both Pentecostals and others) realize that Classical Pentecostals major on the *charismatic* aspects in the book of Acts; after all, this is their "distinctive." To deny this would be like denying that cessationists believe that the gifts have ceased.

I believe (and shall attempt to prove) that Luke says comparatively little about tongues as opposed to salvation in the context of the entire book of Acts. In some books on this issue by tongues-as-evidence proponents, you'd get the impression that Luke spoke of little else. To establish my premise, I shall supply some indicative comments by tongues-as-evidence proponents. But, before I do, let me illustrate what the "straw man" argument is for those who may be a bit fuzzy on the concept.

The Straw Man Fallacy

The "straw man" argument (also called the "straw man fallacy") is the attempt by some unscholarly (and sometimes unscrupulous) people to paint a false picture of their opponent's argument. They attack an argument which is either different from, or at least weaker than, their opponent's best argument. After they paint the false picture and make it look bad, then they say that it should be rejected because it is wrong. Well, of course the argument that *they painted* should be rejected. *It is wrong.* The problem is, however, that their opponents do not believe what they charge them with. A colleague gave this illustration: If you made a cardboard cutout of the present heavyweight boxing champion, you could go up to it and knock it down with ease. Then, you could tell people, "See, I'm tougher than the heavyweight boxing champion." But, the cardboard cutout is just a "straw man." Let's see you do that with the real heavyweight boxing champion.

The Question

The question still remains: "Do tongues-as-evidence proponents really minor on a topic that Luke majored on?" And, the reverse should be asked as well: "Do tongues-as-evidence proponents really major on a topic that Luke only minors on?" How shall we make this determination? In the next chapter, I develop my argument that Luke's emphasis throughout the book of Acts is predominantly soteriological. But in this chapter, I am merely pointing out that tongues-as-evidence proponents emphasize the pneumatological (i.e., charismatic, not soteriological) nature of the book of Acts.

How can we prove that the tongues-as-evidence proponents major on the charismatic aspects rather than the salvation aspects within the book of Acts? To do so, we must let the tongues-as-evidence proponents speak for themselves.

Roger Stronstad

Roger Stronstad is a fine scholar and a tongues-as-evidence proponent. Stronstad is without question one of the most well-known proponents of this position, and he speaks for most Classical Pentecostals on this topic. In fact, he served as the president for the Society for Pentecostal Studies in 1994; he is an adjunct faculty member for the Assemblies of God Theological Seminary, and he is the Academic Dean of Western Pentecostal Bible College, Abbotsford, BC. He is so representative of the Classical Pentecostal position that on the Assemblies of God web site, under *Assemblies of God Beliefs*, it states that for those interested in learning more about this issue "we recommend Roger Stronstad's *The Charismatic Theology of St. Luke* (Hendrickson, 1984)."[1] So, staying with *their recommendation*, we shall consider some representative statements from his text.

In his book, *The Charismatic Theology of St. Luke*, Stronstad deals with the various portions of Scripture from the book of Acts that deal with the Holy Spirit baptism accounts. I shall also deal with these same accounts in the next chapter as I attempt to develop Luke's intent.

In response to James D. G. Dunn's argument that the Holy Spirit reception is soteriological[2] and it should be viewed as such in Acts chapter eight, Roger Stronstad states:

> For Luke, the gift of the Spirit has a vocational purpose and equips the disciples for service. Thus, it is *devoid of any soteriological connotations* and, contra Dunn, it does not mean that "it is God's giving of the Spirit which makes a man a Christian" (emphasis added).[3]

Now, while Stronstad's response to Dunn is in regard to Dunn's interpretation of the Samaritans' reception of the gift of the Spirit in Acts chapter eight—and so I do not want to read too much into Stronstad's words—Stronstad seems to imply that Luke's concept of the gift of the Spirit extends beyond just this passage. His words *"devoid of any soteriological connotations"* are strong indeed. With Stronstad, I too see that the gift of the Spirit has a vocational purpose, and it equips disciples for service. After all, Jesus said that it would be so:

> But you will receive power when the Holy Spirit comes on you; and you will be my witnesses in Jerusalem, and in all Judea and Samaria, and to the ends of the earth (Acts 1:8).

Stronstad further says,

> The gift of the Spirit to the believers at Samaria demonstrates that all, even a despised group like the Samaritans, are to engage in the missionary task.[4]

While I would not disagree with Stronstad's statement entirely, I personally believe that it would be more Lukan to say:

> The gift of the Spirit to the believers at Samaria demonstrates that all, even a despised group like the Samaritans, can be saved. Once saved, they, like all believers, are to engage in the missionary task.

Next, Stronstad deals with the Acts 9 narrative of the gift of the Spirit to Saul (the apostle Paul). He says:

> This narrative brings together two characteristic Lukan motifs: vocational ability and the gift of the Spirit. In describing Saul's encounter with the risen Lord Luke emphasizes his calling *not conversion*. The stress falls upon what Saul must do, to bear the name of Jesus before the Gentiles (emphasis mine).[5]

That Luke describes Saul's calling is without doubt. But, does the *stress* fall upon that call? More shall be said about this in the next chapter. For now, my point is only this: Where does *Stronstad's* emphasis fall? Is it soteriological? Obviously not. Am I developing a "straw man" by simply stating that tongues-as-evidence proponents major on the pneumatological (i.e., charismatic not soteriological) aspects within Acts? Have not Stronstad's words concurred with my statement?

In dealing with the Acts 10 account of the gift of the Spirit to the household of Cornelius, Stronstad says that there is one "inescapable conclusion": that the gift of the Spirit to them has the "same vocational or charismatic purpose as the gift of the Spirit" did for the disciples on the day of Pentecost.[6] While Stronstad does mention the issue of salvation in this context, he does so only in passing: "The outpouring of the Spirit teaches them a new lesson, namely, that God's impartiality applies to more than just salvation, it applies to all His gifts."[7] Then he goes on to say:

> ... the outpouring of the Spirit is dramatic testimony to Cornelius and his household that God makes no distinction between himself [i.e., Cornelius] and the Jews: that is, that they can receive the prophetic gift of the Spirit without having to convert to Judaism.[8]

Again, I think Stronstad is onto something. However, all I am asking is what is *Stronstad's* emphasis here? Does he say of this passage that God is pointing out that even the Gentiles can be saved? No. He says that Luke is emphasizing that they too can receive the prophetic gift of the Spirit.

I show in the next chapter that the Cornelius account in Acts 10 is dramatic testimony to hardheaded and exclusive Jews that "God has granted even the Gentiles *repentance unto life*" (emphasis added, Acts 11:18). Thus, Luke's emphasis is (and ours should be) upon the soteriological connotations of this event. This is not to leave out the vocational or charismatic purpose of the gift of the Spirit; it is, rather, to place the emphasis upon what the inspired author placed it upon. If I have misrepresented the tongues-as-evidence proponents on this point, you could not prove it from Stronstad's own writings.

Other Tongues-as-Evidence Voices

According to Gary B. McGee, D. W. Kerr was an articulate spokesman for the Classical Pentecostal doctrine that speaking in tongues is the initial, physical evidence of the baptism in the Holy Spirit.[9] D. W. Kerr, writing in the *Pentecostal Evangel Magazine*, the official Assemblies of God publication, stated that Luke had voluminous material from which to write the book of Acts. Luke, then, selected what he wanted in the book for emphasis' sake. And, what was it that Luke was emphasizing? Well, according to Kerr, "they that believe shall speak in tongues."[10] So, Luke was operating as a compiler/editor/writer. Kerr points out that the apostle John did this as well. He says that John, "made a *selection* of just such materials as served his purpose, and that is, to confirm believers in the faith concerning Jesus Christ the son of God."[11] Likewise, then, according to Kerr, Luke makes his selection from the voluminous materials to serve his purpose of establishing his own emphasis, which, according to Kerr is that *those who believe shall speak in tongues.*[12] Then, with regard to speaking in tongues in the book of Acts, Kerr says, "Is this not an altogether striking characteristic of the book of Acts?"[13] It seems evident where Kerr's emphasis is. It is non-soteriological.

While I would say that it is not *an altogether striking* characteristic of the book of Acts, since that would seem to make it unique and speaking in tongues is mentioned elsewhere in the Bible, it is nonetheless an obvious characteristic in the book of Acts. But, more striking is Luke's continual emphasis on salvation, as we shall see in the next chapter.

Donald A. Johns, former Associate Professor and Chairperson of the Bible and Theology Department at the Assemblies of God Theological Seminary, says: "Luke emphasizes Spirit-empowered ministry, but largely ignores both the ethical aspects of the Spirit in the believer and the role of the Spirit in conversion."[14]

That Luke emphasizes Spirit-empowered ministry in the book of Acts is not in question here. Of course he does. But, did he *largely ignore the role of the Spirit in conversion*? I think not. Again, the point I am attempting to establish is that tongues-as-evidence proponents *themselves* emphasize the non-soteriological aspects of Luke's writings in the book of Acts. Donald A. Johns also states:

> In sum, we might say that Luke is concerned with believers being "baptized" in the Spirit, initiated into the powerful charismatic service, but Luke is even more concerned with the service itself.[15]

I agree in part with Johns. Luke is certainly concerned with the baptism in the Holy Spirit and powerful charismatic service. However, I doubt that a summary of Luke's intent should put those aspects ahead of his intent to show the progression of salvation throughout the book of Acts.

Again, my question is simple: What is it that the tongues-as-evidence proponents emphasize? Is Luke's emphasis on salvation, or is it upon the baptism in the Holy Spirit and powerful charismatic service?

Douglas A. Oss is professor of hermeneutics and New Testament at Central Bible College of the Assemblies of God. In the terrific book, *Are Miraculous Gifts for Today? Four Views*, Oss clearly sets up Luke's intent as he sees it:

> Beginning with Jesus' command to the disciples in Acts 1:5 to wait for the baptism in the Holy Spirit (cf. Luke 3:16), we see that Luke's emphasis is on the empowering work of the Spirit for witness. Spirit baptism in Acts is not defined in terms of regeneration/ sanctification but in terms of power for witness (Acts 1:8).[16]

I don't want to belabor this point, but more than that, I don't want there to be any doubt about the Classical Pentecostal position here. According to the Classical Pentecostal position, Luke's emphasis in Acts is *not* defined in terms of regeneration. It is, rather, about the empowering charismatic work of the Spirit. Oss continues:

> Repentance and baptism in the name of Jesus indeed bring salvation (2:38), but Luke is careful to emphasize the empowering work of the Spirit rather than inner transformation.[17]

Oss could not be more clear. He says that Luke is *careful* to emphasize the empowering work of the Spirit *rather than* the soteriological inner transformation. As I said earlier, I am surprised that anyone would question that Classical Pentecostals major on the Holy Spirit's charismatic activity in the book of Acts rather than the soteriological aspects found therein.

Oss further states, "Merely to equate Luke's presentation with Pauline regeneration is to lose a vital dimension of the New Testament witness to the work of the Spirit in the church."[18] While I would agree with Oss at this point, my reason for using his words here is to show that his emphasis is not on soteriological issues concerning Luke's intent.

Then, Oss makes this declarative statement in representation of Pentecostals: "Pentecostals, then, read Acts against the background of anointing for witness and service rather than regeneration."[19] This is astonishingly clear and supports my premise.

Earlier I said that I was not arguing that Classical Pentecostals entirely miss Luke's soteriological intent, but that they major on the charismatic aspects in the book of Acts and minor on Luke's soteriology. What is Luke's intent, his "agenda"? I have argued that the Classical Pentecostal sees Luke's intent as charismatic and not soteriological. Oss, once again in his clear and precise way, agrees.

> Regeneration is most certainly not excluded in Luke's pneumatology; to argue that would

be to argue from silence.[20] Simply put, Luke's narrative expresses his own distinctive theological agenda—the Spirit's charismatic anointing.[21]

So, Luke's "own distinctive theological agenda" (intent) as seen by Classical Pentecostals is the *Spirit's charismatic anointing*, so they themselves say.

Summary

My point in supplying these *indicative quotes*—and many more could be added but it would simply be overkill—is to establish that the tongues-as-evidence proponents are *very clear*, and in many cases *very adamant*, that Luke's emphasis (intent, agenda) throughout the book of Acts is non-soteriological. Their emphasis rests, rather, in the charismatic aspect of the baptism in the Holy Spirit and the supposedly necessary corollary, speaking in tongues.

Again, and I want to make sure that this is clear, I am not saying nor implying that all tongues-as-evidence proponents miss Luke's soteriological intent in Acts. As stated before, Classical Pentecostals do see in Acts many soteriological passages. This is obvious. No one is saying that they do not. What *I am* saying, however, is that they do not *major* on Luke's soteriological intent. They major rather on the charismatic aspect of the baptism in the Holy Spirit; whereas I believe that Luke majors on soteriology. This fact will be established in the next chapter.[22]

In researching the Classical Pentecostals' emphasis

concerning Luke's intent in Acts, what I have found is that not only do Classical Pentecostals emphasize the charismatic rather than the soteriological aspects of Luke's writings, they do so with unabashed vigor.

End Notes

[1] Specifically this is found under the title, "Questions about the Baptism in the Holy Spirit"—"Is the Book of Acts intended to be history or theology, and can doctrine be based on less than declarative statements?" Accessed via Internet, July 10, 2002, at http://www.ag.org/top/beliefs/position_papers/4185_spirit-filled_life_faq.cfm#1.

[2] See, James D. G. Dunn, *Baptism in the Holy Spirit: A Re-examination of the New Testament Teaching of the Gift of the Spirit in relation to Pentecostalism today*, Studies in Biblical Theology, Second Series, 15 (London: SCM Press Ltd. 1970).

[3] Roger Stronstad, *The Charismatic Theology of St. Luke* (Peabody, MA.: Hendrickson Publishers, Inc., 1984), p. 64.

[4] Ibid., p. 65.

[5] Ibid., p. 66.

[6] Ibid., p. 67.

[7] Ibid.

[8] Ibid.

[9] Gary B. McGee, editor, *Initial Evidence: Historical and Biblical Perspectives on the Pentecostal Doctrine of Spirit Baptism*, "Early Pentecostal Hermeneutics: Tongues as Evidence in the Book of Acts" (Peabody, MA.: Hendrickson Publishers, Inc., 1991), p. 104.

[10] As quoted by Gary B. McGee in *Initial Evidence*, p. 104.

[11] Ibid.

[12] Ibid.

[13] Ibid.

[14] Ibid., Donald A. Johns, "Some New Directions in the Hermeneutics of Classical Pentecostalism's Doctrine of Initial Evidence," p. 149.

[15] Ibid., p. 164.

[16] Douglas A. Oss, "A Pentecostal/Charismatic View" in *Are Miraculous Gifts for Today? Four Views*, Wayne A. Grudem, gen. ed., (Grand Rapids: Zondervan Publishing House, 1996), pp. 253-254.

[17] Ibid., pp. 254-255.

[18] Ibid., p. 256.

[19] Ibid., p. 257.

[20] Oss states that to argue that regeneration is excluded in Luke's pneumatology is to argue from silence, by which he means that Luke's pneumatology is silent on this issue. However, all throughout the book of Acts, Luke

is certainly not silent at all. This shall be clearly seen in the next chapter.

[21] Ibid.

[22] There was no lack of Classical Pentecostal statements to quote for this chapter establishing the fact that the Classical Pentecostals major on the charismatic aspect of the baptism in the Holy Spirit and speaking in tongues as opposed to the soteriological aspects of Luke's writings in Acts. In fact, it was difficult to limit this chapter to so few quotes. But, I did not wish to belabor a point that is obvious to so many. So, I simply selected indicative quotations by well-known individuals and publications that would fairly represent the Classical Pentecostal position as a whole.

Chapter 5

Argument # 1: Authorial Intent

What Was Luke Trying to Convey?

Of all the arguments opposing the initial, physical evidence of the baptism in the Holy Spirit, that of *authorial intent* is, without a doubt, the most convincing for this researcher. Once this is clearly seen, the other arguments serve to support the conclusion and further tip the scales of circumstantial evidence.

Authorial intent deals with the entire book of Acts; thus, it covers a broader biblical scope than any other single argument. It is important to do a thoughtful exegetical consideration throughout the entire book of Acts with regard to this question. While some arguments against the position have to do with certain rules of logic or hermeneutics, authorial intent has to do with searching the Scriptures themselves rather than attempting simply to apply certain rules of logic or hermeneutics (both of which may have exceptions).

The Principle of Guiding Questions

In hermeneutics as well as in scientific inquiry, we are taught to ask "guiding questions." A guiding question is posed by the inquirer and is meant to focus the research. For example, if your science professor told you to look at the sky through your telescope on a particular night and look for something, you'd ask, "What exactly is it that you want me to look for?"

Let's say that there was a specific crater on the moon that would be visible that night, but unless he "guided" you to look first at the moon, and then more precisely at a certain section of the moon, you might be searching the heavens for hours looking at various stars and planets without a clue as to what your celestial inquiry is supposed to lead you to. In fact, with the heavens being as vast as they are, you might arrive in class the next day and announce that you saw many things that were not even related to the moon. So, we must "focus" our attention to a certain "location" or subject.

We have all approached the Bible without guiding questions. We usually do this during our devotion times. We enter that reading without "guiding questions" to focus our attention because we are not looking for any one thing in particular. During those times, we are "just reading" to spend time in the Word. But, all of us have also spent time "looking" for something in particular. I remember once wanting to know exactly how many miracles Jesus performed in the four Gospels, and how many and which ones were unique to each book. So, I had my guiding questions of inquiry for that study.

1. How many miracles did Jesus perform in the four Gospels?

2. How many and which ones are unique to each of the four Gospels?

Bible students should develop the ability to ask well-defined guiding questions that will focus their research without imposing a forced grid. They should also develop the ability to clarify their ideas that are influencing and guiding the inquiry and understand how those ideas compare with current biblical knowledge. Students must learn to formulate questions, design and execute investigations, interpret data, communicate conclusions based on the evidence, propose alternative explanations, and critique prior conclusions and procedures. With the foregoing as a base, let's establish our "guiding question" for this chapter.

Our Guiding Question

Our guiding question is this: "What importance does Luke give to tongues as evidence of the baptism in the Holy Spirit?" For this is the key to understanding authorial intent with regard to this issue. Since Luke is the inspired writer of the book of Acts, and since it is the book of Acts that depicts the baptism in the Holy Spirit and speaking in tongues, it is important to understand his intent.

Some may demur precisely at this point and argue that it is arrogant for one to claim to know the intent of another. Yet, isn't this exactly what the opponents claim? If they claim that my position is wrong about Luke's intent, then is it not their claim, even if only implied, to know Luke's intent? What other possible grounds could they hold to make such a charge? And, if they do not themselves claim to know Luke's intent, then how can they say that my idea of his intent is incorrect? In the final analysis, the point is this: Does the evidence I provide in this book demonstrate Luke's true intent?

And, you, the reader, will look at the evidence that I shall give, and you will have to determine if I have *discovered* and *demonstrated* Luke's intent concerning our topic of investigation.

With the groundwork now laid, it is time to proceed to the text, i.e., the book of Acts, and to look at *authorial intent*.

The Jesus View
Acts 1:4-8

> On one occasion, while he was eating with them, he gave them this command: "Do not leave Jerusalem, but wait for *the gift my Father promised*, which you have heard me speak about. For John baptized with water, but in a few days you will be *baptized with the Holy Spirit*." So when they met together, they asked him, "Lord, are you at this time going to restore the kingdom to Israel?" He said to them: "It is not for you to know the times or dates the Father has set by his own authority. But you will receive power when the Holy Spirit comes on you; and you will be my witnesses in Jerusalem, and in all Judea and Samaria, and to the ends of the earth" (emphasis added).

Jesus tells His disciples that they are to wait in Jerusalem for the gift of the Father (v. 4), which is the Holy Spirit (i.e., "baptized with the Holy Spirit," v. 5). It is important to note that Jesus himself made the connection between the "gift my Father promised" and "baptized in the Holy Spirit."

The Purpose of the Promised Holy Spirit

The purpose of this promised Holy Spirit is power. The power of God that came upon the disciples due to the infilling with the Holy Spirit was the awesome life-giving power of God.

Note verse 8: "you will receive *power* when the Holy Spirit comes on you"; this is obviously a reference to the baptism in the Holy Spirit. Many Classical Pentecostals pause at this point and rejoice in the glory of these words and at the prospect of such an event. However, if we stop here, we will miss the purpose of this power. Verse 8b says that the purpose of this *power* is that they will be Christ's *witnesses* in Jerusalem, in all Judea and Samaria, and to the ends of the earth. From the outset of the book of Acts, Luke says that the baptism in the Holy Spirit and the consequent power of God that will be given to the disciples is inexorably linked to being His witnesses. Luke's intent is clear, even at this early stage in the book; it is to emphasize evangelism (a soteriological point). Of course, at this point the emphasize is twofold: not only is it soteriological (evangelism), it is also about the charismatic *power* of the Holy Spirit which equips the disciples to be His witnesses.

The One Hundred Twenty
Acts 2: 1-4

> When the day of Pentecost came, they were all together in one place. Suddenly a sound like the blowing of a violent wind came from heaven and filled the whole house where they were sitting. They saw what seemed to be tongues of fire that separated and came to rest on each of them. All of them were filled with the Holy Spirit and began to speak in other tongues as the Spirit enabled them.

In Acts 2:1-4, Luke records that the disciples (i.e., the 120) were filled with the Holy Spirit. In this particular situation, there seems to be a clear *modus operandi*. (1) The disciples were believers (thus saved); (2) they were baptized in the Holy Spirit; and (3) they spoke in tongues. Every Classical Pentecostal can point this out, and non-Pentecostals are simply arguing against the facts if they deny this sequence.

Some have argued that these disciples were not saved until the day of Pentecost when they were filled with the Holy Spirit. However, one might simply ask, had one of the disciples died prior to the day of Pentecost, would he have gone to hell? Certainly not. If one would say yes, then another simple question may be helpful. Why would the thief on the cross be saved and Jesus' disciples not? Obviously, the idea that the disciples were not saved prior to the infilling with the Holy Spirit on the day of Pentecost is a non-biblical one. Thus, non-Pentecostals who are frightened to see a *modus operandi* in this text would do well not to argue against the facts, but rather they should simply point out that one historical narrative does not make a doctrine (or a normative pattern).

However, *modus operandi* notwithstanding, what is Luke *intending* his reader to understand by this passage of Scripture? First, Luke has not yet finished his recounting of what transpired. Thus, if one stops at this point and majors on just these verses, he will be making the mistake of taking these passages out of context.

Luke goes on to say that some people were wondering what all of these phenomena were about. Luke says that Peter stood up and addressed the crowd and said that the outward manifestation of tongues that they had witnessed was the fulfillment of Joel's eschatological prophecy that the Holy Spirit would be given (poured out, v. 17) to God's people in the last days. In concluding his quote from Joel, Peter ends with the words, "And everyone who calls upon the name of the Lord will be saved" (v. 21). The words "will be saved" are Luke's soteriological emphasis.

Power to Be Witnesses

Interestingly, Luke makes it clear that Jesus told His disciples that the infilling with the Holy Spirit would give the disciples power to be His *witnesses* (1:8), and in the very first account of the baptism of the Holy Spirit Luke clearly states how Peter, the one who had earlier denied his Lord due to fear and self-preservation, boldly proclaimed the gospel of Christ to thousands of people. Peter had received the baptism in the Holy Spirit and the *power* to be His witness. What could be more clear? In other words, Luke is pointing out that Jesus said a particular thing would happen, and it happened just as he said it would. This is no mere coincidental connection. It is causal. Luke has a point that he wants to portray, and that point is soteriological in nature. Thus, the baptism in the Holy Spirit is linked, in Luke's thinking, to the ability to bring about a soteriological emphasis, albeit within a Spirit-empowered vocational ability.

It would be a mistake to deny that tongues were the outward manifestation of the infilling of the Holy Spirit in Acts 2:4ff. However, one must be careful not to assign *a greater significance* to tongues than Luke does. A hermeneutical axiom is that a passage of straight prose[1] cannot mean something that the author and his readers would not have understood. Likewise one must not read a *foreign intent* into the *author's intent*. While tongues are spoken of by Luke and identified as a phenomenon that occurred, his point so far, and thus his emphasis, is soteriological—through Spirit-empowered vocational service.

Did Three Thousand Speak in Tongues?
Acts 2:38-41

> Peter replied, "Repent and be baptized, every one of you, in the name of Jesus Christ for the forgiveness of your sins. And you will receive the gift of the Holy Spirit. The promise is for you and your children and for all who are far off—for all whom the Lord our God will call." With many other words he warned them; and he pleaded with them, "Save yourselves from this corrupt generation." Those who accepted

his message were baptized, and about three thousand were added to their number that day.

In this passage, there is an account of three thousand people coming to faith in Jesus Christ. These were baptized in water as an outward demonstration of their newfound faith in Jesus Christ. Please note that Luke clearly records Peter's words to these people. Peter states that if they will repent and be baptized in the name of Jesus Christ for the forgiveness of their sins, then they too "will receive the gift of the Holy Spirit" (v. 38-39). These people had just witnessed the outpouring of the Holy Spirit upon the 120 disciples, and they wondered out loud what this all meant. Peter sums it up and says, "God has raised this Jesus to life, and we are all witnesses of the fact. Exalted to the right hand of God, he has received from the Father the promised Holy Spirit and has poured out what you now *see and hear*" (emphasis added, Acts 2:32-33).

They had *seen* and *heard* some outward manifestations of the Spirit's presence: (1) "a sound like the blowing of a violent wind," (2) tongues of fire that came to rest on each of the 120, and (3) the utterance of tongues. It is not clear if all three thousand heard and saw all three of these phenomena, but it seems clear that they did all hear them speaking in tongues—"When they heard this sound, a crowd came together in bewilderment, because each one heard them speaking in his own language" (Acts 2:6).

Peter said that they would receive this same *gift of the Holy Spirit* if they repented and were baptized in the name of Jesus for the forgiveness of their sins. And, they did repent. Luke says, "Those who accepted his message were baptized, and about three thousand were added to their number that day" (Acts 2:41).

However, even though Luke clearly states that a significant number of people (three thousand!) came to faith in Jesus Christ that day (this is soteriological), he does not say that they spoke in tongues. There seem to be two arguments that Pentecostals have proposed which attempt to explain why Luke does not mention that any of these three thousand spoke in tongues (which would be pneumatological).

Not Baptized

The first argument, and the weakest, is that none of the three thousand were baptized in the Holy Spirit that day; they were only saved, but not "Spirit-baptized," and that's why Luke does not mention it. Of course this conclusion is certainly not in keeping with what was transpiring on this remarkable day in the history of the church of Jesus Christ.

It would be incredible to believe that only hours (perhaps minutes) after the descent of the Holy Spirit upon the 120 in the upper room that none of these three thousand people received the baptism in the Holy Spirit. After all, that is *exactly* what Peter (under inspiration of the Holy Spirit) said would happen if they repented and were baptized in the name of Jesus Christ for the forgiveness of their sins. They did repent. They were water baptized. Logic demands (and Luke's account implies) that they did, therefore, also receive the "gift of the Holy Spirit," i.e., they were baptized in the Holy Spirit.

It's Just Not Recorded

The second argument says, logically so, that they did receive the "gift of the Holy Spirit," i.e., they were baptized in the Holy Spirit. However, this argument goes on to conclude that they all spoke in tongues as the initial, physical evidence of this baptism, and that Luke just does not record the outward phenomena because it is implied in the text. Stanley Horton argues for this position. And, he supplies a "reason" for Luke's omission of this outward phenomenon of speaking in tongues as the initial, physical evidence of the baptism in the Holy Spirit. He says that Luke did not have the space to record it in the book of Acts.[2] Interestingly, the process by which Horton has concluded that Luke did not have the space to record the details in this book is not given. Without an explanation of that process, one is left with the conclusion that it is simply Horton's assumption. And, this is just the sort of *assumption* that non-Pentecostals attack as simply an eisegesis of the text to arrive at a preconceived conclusion. What possible evidence could this conclusion be based on, other than the fact that it plays well into Classical Pentecostals' final conclusion?

Horton also concludes that all 3,000 received the promise of the Father as Peter said they would and that they were filled with the Spirit. With this, I fully agree. To deny this would be to go against the very clear implications of Peter's message. Thus, *this* conclusion is based upon the Scripture.

However, Horton then goes on to say that *we can be sure that all three thousand also spoke* in other tongues as did the 120 in Acts 2:4.[3] Again, Horton gives a conclusion based not upon Scripture but upon his "control belief" about how the reception of the Holy Spirit is manifested. But, let's be clear on this point. The passage does not say they spoke in tongues, and Luke does not imply that they did.

A ubiquitous argument by Classical Pentecostals that allows them to "be sure that *all three thousand also spoke* in other tongues" is the idea that Luke does not need to mention speaking in tongues in every case or even in most cases because it was simply so common that it was taken for granted. So, they go on to assume that when people were filled with the Holy Spirit, those people then spoke in tongues. This was, they argue, the common occurrence and thus there was no need for a continual verbal confirmation of the manifestation of speaking in tongues. But upon what is this argument based? It is based upon the Classical Pentecostal premise that all who are filled (i.e., baptized) in the Holy Spirit will speak in tongues. In other words, it is a circular argument. They state that speaking in tongues as evidence was so common that Luke need not mention it. But, how do they know that it was so common if Luke hardly mentions it? This is simply a case of begging the question.

However, even if Horton were correct and indeed all three thousand converts spoke in tongues that day as a result of the baptism in the Holy Spirit, what both

Pentecostals and non-Pentecostals must realize is that this is not the present issue facing us with regard to authorial intent. This takes us back to our **Guiding Question:** "What *importance* does Luke give to tongues as evidence of the baptism in the Holy Spirit?"

The issue is not, "Did the three thousand speak in tongues?" The issue is, *"Why does Luke not make a point of saying that they did (or did not) speak in tongues?"* He does not mention it because it is not an issue. What Luke does take the time and space to describe is the *soteriological* outcome on this unique day.

What is at issue for Luke is establishing that Jesus Christ is the means of salvation and that people were coming to faith in Christ; he is not attempting to establish a *paradigm* about tongues as the initial, physical evidence of the baptism in the Holy Spirit. Whether or not the three thousand spoke in tongues does not matter. If it had mattered, Luke would have certainly made that clear. Researchers must take their cue as to the importance of this question from the inspired author of the book, and he does not mention if three thousand spoke in tongues or if they did not. If it were as important an issue as Classical Pentecostals say it is, Luke would have used this three-thousand-person example to develop the concept. But, he does not.

Luke was a theologian, and he was presenting theology as well as a historical account. The question is, what theology was he presenting? Certainly he was presenting a soteriological theology and a pneumatological one. But, was he attempting to establish within that pneumatological theology that speaking in tongues is the initial, physical evidence of the baptism in the Holy Spirit? If so, then this event would have been a paradigmatic gold mine. Three thousand people *on the day of Pentecost* received the baptism in the Holy Spirit, yet Luke does not so much as whisper that they did or that they did not speak in tongues! Why? What was his emphasis? Certainly it was not "tongues as evidence." For if it had been, then Luke was a very poor communicator. But Luke had no trouble at all communicating to the reader that three thousand people came to glorious saving faith in Jesus Christ, the Messiah. Even if they did all speak in tongues, it is interesting that Luke *does not feel that it was important enough* to say so.

The issue then is not whether they spoke in tongues. The issue is that Luke chose not to say if they did, and so exegetes must conclude that Luke's intent for his reader was something *other than* the issue of establishing a pattern of tongues as evidence, at least at this stage. Actually, it is quite simple: If Luke had intended to show that speaking in tongues was the initial, physical evidence of the baptism in the Holy Spirit, he would have.

Luke's Emphasis

Classical Pentecostals place great emphasis upon the issue of establishing a pattern of tongues as evidence while Luke, at least so far, places no emphasis upon it. If anyone had the divine authority to establish an emphasis on this issue, certainly it was Luke (and Paul, as we shall see later). Yet he does not do this at all. His emphasis is predominantly soteriological.

Some Pentecostals have taken their emphasis to great extremes. The wife of a colleague, a Classical-Pentecostal pastor, once chided me for my lack of emphasis upon tongues as the initial, physical evidence of the baptism in the Holy Spirit. She asked me, "Don't you think that we should preach the gospel of tongues as much as we preach the gospel of salvation in Christ?" First, the New Testament does not speak of some supposed "gospel of tongues." That is precisely the point. The New Testament does not elevate the tongues issue as highly as all that. Luke does not vigorously emphasize it (as he does the message of salvation and the fact that people were coming to Christ), though he had many opportunities to do so, and none of the other New Testament writers give it the supreme place that many in the Classical Pentecostal tradition do. While tongues should not be elevated above the level given to it in the text of Scripture, neither should tongues be relegated to a supposedly closed dispensation. Neither extreme is scriptural.

In conclusion of this passage and its implications for this argument, it is time to recapitulate. On the day of Pentecost, 120 disciples spoke in tongues as the Holy Spirit filled each of them. Three thousand others on the *same day* accepted Jesus Christ as their Messiah, were water baptized, and received the baptism in the Holy Spirit, yet Luke is completely silent about them speaking in tongues. It was simply not his intent to convey tongues as the initial, physical evidence of the baptism in the Holy Spirit. If it had been, he would have done so.

Added to Their Number Daily
Acts 2:46-47

> Every day they continued to meet together in the temple courts. They broke bread in their homes and ate together with glad and sincere hearts, praising God and enjoying the favor of all the people. And the Lord added to their number daily those who were being saved.

God added more to the church daily, and yet Luke does not say anything about speaking in tongues. Luke has already established by recording Peter's message that those who believe in Jesus Christ *will receive the gift of the Holy Spirit*; thus, it is safe to infer that those who were being added to the church daily were in fact receiving the Holy Spirit. This is the same hermeneutical assumption that was made in Acts 2:41 with regard to the three thousand. We have a biblical *right of inference* because the Scripture records that Peter *explicitly* stated that this would be so in his sermonic instruction:

> Peter replied, "Repent and be baptized, every one of you, in the name of Jesus Christ for the forgiveness of your sins. And you will receive the gift of the Holy Spirit. The promise is for you and your children and for all who are far off—for all whom the Lord our God will call" (Acts 2:38-39).

However, as in the case of the three thousand, one cannot simply assume that they spoke in tongues. There is no explicit statement giving interpreters the *right of inference* in this regard. Peter did not say: *"Repent and be baptized, every one of you, in the name of Jesus Christ for the forgiveness of your sins. And you will receive the gift of speaking in tongues."*

What one sees clearly, however, is that once again Luke is emphasizing salvation, and he is silent about tongues. So far Luke has recorded three occasions in which people were either receiving the outpouring of the Holy Spirit or they were repenting and coming to Christ, which by biblical implication means that they too were receiving the promise of the Father, i.e., the Holy Spirit. The number of Holy-Spirit recipients on these three occasions exceeds three thousand people, and yet Luke mentions tongues-speaking with regard to only 120 people.

Again, it is important to point out that this does not prove that none of the others spoke in tongues. Luke simply does not say if they did or not. It should be growing clearer that Luke is far more concerned about reporting that people are coming to Christ than he is about emphasizing if they spoke in tongues or not. One does not have to conclude (yet) that tongues is not the initial, physical evidence of the baptism in the Holy Spirit. However, one should conclude that Luke is not making tongues a central theme or issue in the Acts account. Thus far, the authorial intent is clearly, and predominantly, soteriological in nature.

Peter Filled with the Holy Spirit
Acts 4:8-13

Then Peter, filled with the Holy Spirit, said to

them: "Rulers and elders of the people! If we are being called to account today for an act of kindness shown to a cripple and are asked how he was healed, then know this, you and all the people of Israel: It is by the name of Jesus Christ of Nazareth, whom you crucified but whom God raised from the dead, that this man stands before you healed. He is 'the stone you builders rejected, which has become the capstone.' Salvation is found in no one else, for there is no other name under heaven given to men by which we must be saved." When they saw the courage of Peter and John and realized that they were unschooled, ordinary men, they were astonished and they took note that these men had been with Jesus.

In this passage, Luke says that Peter was "filled with the Holy Spirit." He makes no mention of tongues here; in fact, it appears that Peter was filled with the Holy Spirit and proclaimed a salvation message with courage (v. 13). However, as Classical Pentecostals point out, this passage is not speaking of the same thing that transpired on the day of Pentecost nor that transpires when one is newly saved and filled with the Holy Spirit. However, this passage is mentioned here because the term "filled with the Holy Spirit" is used therein. This text will be discussed again later.

All Filled with the Holy Spirit
Acts 4:31

After they prayed, the place where they were

meeting was shaken. And they were all filled with the Holy Spirit and spoke the word of God boldly.

Here, Luke says that some disciples were "filled with the Holy Spirit and [they] spoke the word of God boldly." He makes no mention of tongues here. However, this account, like the one immediately above, is not speaking of the same thing that transpired on the day of Pentecost nor that transpires when one is newly saved and filled with the Holy Spirit.

More Men and Women Believed
Acts 5:14

> Nevertheless, more and more men and women believed in the Lord and were added to their number.

In this passage, Luke says that "more and more men and women believed in the Lord and were added to their number." Notice the two points that Luke is making here. First, he says that "more and more men and women believed in the Lord." Again, Luke, true to his intent, is showing his readers that the central theme is salvation. Second, his words "and were added to their number" indicates that Luke is interested in showing that the church was growing. Yet he makes no mention of tongues. Some have assumed that these people were not being baptized in the Holy Spirit. However, such an assumption is gratuitous. Peter had explained the divinely established pattern. He said that those who would repent and be baptized in the name of Jesus for the forgiveness of their sins would receive the gift of the Holy Spirit. Now, would Luke say that "more and more men and women believed in the Lord and were added to their number" if they had not repented and come to the Lord? Of course not. Thus, it is safe to assume that these people also received the gift of the Holy Spirit. Yet, speaking in tongues is not mentioned. Again, this does not mean that they did not speak in tongues. At this point, all that is being shown is that Luke *is not* emphasizing speaking in tongues as a constitutive element of the Holy Spirit reception experience.

The Number of Disciples Was Increasing
Acts 6:1

> In those days when the number of disciples was increasing, the Grecian Jews among them complained against the Hebraic Jews because their widows were being overlooked in the daily distribution of food.

Here Luke says that the number of the disciples was increasing. Yet, again, he makes no mention of speaking in tongues. Interestingly, something as supposedly important as speaking in tongues is not mentioned, but an issue of the daily distribution of food is mentioned.

A Large Number of Priests Became Obedient
Acts 6:7

> So the word of God spread. The number of disciples in Jerusalem increased rapidly, and a large number of priests became obedient to the faith.

A large number of Jewish priests got saved. This would have been an excellent opportunity had Luke wanted to emphasize tongues as the initial, physical evidence of the baptism in the Holy Spirit. After all, Jewish priests getting saved and receiving the promise of the Father, i.e., the Holy Spirit, is a noteworthy fact. It is significant enough that Luke takes the time to point out that "a large number of priests became obedient to the faith." Yet, with this significant fact, he does not go on to say that they spoke in tongues. One may assume that they *did* receive the baptism in the Holy Spirit, but one cannot assume that they spoke in tongues. As argued above, one may assume that they did receive the baptism in the Holy Spirit because Peter clearly explained what one must do to receive the promise of the Father. And, since Luke says that this "large number of priests became *obedient* to the faith," exegetes may assume that they received the gift of the Holy Spirit, just as Peter said they would (Acts 2:38-41). Yet, exegetes cannot also assume that they spoke in tongues because in only one passage up to this point does Luke say that anyone spoke in tongues. Also, up to this point, Scripture does not give us any reason to believe that a *necessary pattern* has been established. Conversely, one also must not arbitrarily assume that they did not speak in tongues. What is sure is this: Luke is *not* emphasizing the issue of tongues, but he *is* emphasizing salvation.

Stephen Full of the Holy Spirit
Acts 7:55-56
But Stephen, full of the Holy Spirit, looked up

to heaven and saw the glory of God, and Jesus standing at the right hand of God. "Look," he said, "I see heaven open and the Son of Man standing at the right hand of God."

Luke says that Stephen was "full of the Holy Spirit." Speaking in tongues is not mentioned. However, this account is not speaking of the same thing that transpired on the day of Pentecost nor that transpires when one is newly saved and filled with the Holy Spirit. Thus, this text is used in the same way as are Acts 4:8 and 4:31 above.

Men and Women Were Baptized
Acts 8:12

> But when they believed Philip as he preached the good news of the kingdom of God and the name of Jesus Christ, they were baptized, both men and women.

More people believed and were baptized. Speaking in tongues is not mentioned. Luke's emphasis here is soteriological.

When Simon Saw
Acts 8:15-23

> When they arrived, they prayed for them that they might receive the Holy Spirit, because the Holy Spirit had not yet come upon any of them; they had simply been baptized into the name of the Lord Jesus. Then Peter and John placed their hands on them, and they

received the Holy Spirit. When Simon saw that the Spirit was given at the laying on of the apostles' hands, he offered them money and said, "Give me also this ability so that everyone on whom I lay my hands may receive the Holy Spirit." Peter answered: "May your money perish with you, because you thought you could buy the gift of God with money! You have no part or share in this ministry, because your heart is not right before God. Repent of this wickedness and pray to the Lord. Perhaps he will forgive you for having such a thought in your heart. For I see that you are full of bitterness and captive to sin."

Classical Pentecostals often argue that though speaking in tongues is not explicitly mentioned in this text (Acts 8:9-24), it is implied. They say that it is implied in verses 18 and 19. Here it says that, "When Simon saw that the Spirit was given at the laying on of the apostles' hands, he offered them money and said, 'Give me also this ability so that everyone on whom I lay my hands may receive the Holy Spirit.'" Notice that verses 12-13 state that some of the Samaritans believed and were baptized. Yet, in verses 14-16, Luke says that the Samaritans had not received the Holy Spirit. So, Peter and John laid their hands on them, prayed for them, and the Samaritans received the Holy Spirit. For the Classical Pentecostal, this passage indicates that the baptism in the Holy Spirit is a subsequent work of grace. Of course, as Horton points out some people argue that the Samaritans were not truly in Jesus until Peter and John came and prayed for them. But, why then would

Philip, a man full of the Spirit and wisdom, have baptized them if their faith was not real?[4] Then, when Simon saw that the Holy Spirit had been given to the Samaritans by the laying on of the apostle's hands, he asked them to sell him the power to lay his hands on people and impart the Holy Spirit to them. It is apparent that Simon saw something, some outward manifestation, and Classical Pentecostals assume that it was speaking in tongues. This seems to be an educated assumption, but there is no way to be positive.

Luke does *not* tell us what it was that Simon actually saw. So, we should be careful not to make a dogmatic statement that it was *in fact* tongues that Simon saw, and we should also be cautioned from stating emphatically that it was not tongues. The only thing that is certain is that Luke *does not say* what the outward manifestation was that captured Simon's attention. Whatever the manifestation was, Luke does not emphasize it, and that is the real point.

Again, if Luke wanted to make an explicit statement about tongues as the initial, physical evidence of the baptism in the Holy Spirit, this would have been an ideal opportunity. Yet Luke passes it by. Remember our guiding question is, "What importance does Luke give to tongues as evidence of the baptism in the Holy Spirit?" In this hotly debated passage, Luke does not mention tongues! Thus, how important was it to him?

It was not Luke's intention to teach what the primary, physical evidence of the baptism in the Holy Spirit was. Perhaps, there is no *single* primary, physical evidence of the baptism in the Holy Spirit. For *if* it had been Luke's intention to teach us what the primary, physical evidence of the baptism in the Holy Spirit was, he certainly did not make it clear.

Philip Baptized Him
Acts 8:36, 38-39

> As they traveled along the road, they came to some water and the eunuch said, "Look, here is water. Why shouldn't I be baptized?" . . . . And he gave orders to stop the chariot. Then both Philip and the eunuch went down into the water and Philip baptized him. When they came up out of the water, the Spirit of the Lord suddenly took Philip away, and the eunuch did not see him again, but went on his way rejoicing.

The Ethiopian eunuch became a believer, was baptized in water, and went on his way rejoicing. There is no mention of speaking in tongues. What is Luke's intent? It is soteriological. When one finishes reading the account of the Ethiopian eunuch, one is absolutely certain that the Ethiopian eunuch got saved.

Saul Filled with the Holy Spirit
Acts 9:17-20

> Then Ananias went to the house and entered it. Placing his hands on Saul, he said, "Brother Saul, the Lord—Jesus, who appeared to you on the road as you were coming here—has sent me so that you may see again and be filled with the Holy Spirit."

> Immediately, something like scales fell from Saul's eyes, and he could see again. He got up and was baptized, and after taking some food, he regained his strength. Saul spent several days with the disciples in Damascus. At once he began to preach in the synagogues that Jesus is the Son of God.

Both Pentecostals and non-Pentecostals use this portion of Scripture to support their views. Pentecostals say that while Luke does not explicitly say that Paul spoke in tongues at this time, Paul himself later (1 Corinthians 14:18) says he spoke in tongues. Non-Pentecostals point to this portion of Scripture to indicate that while Paul was filled with the Holy Spirit, it does not say that he spoke in tongues.

Both arguments seem to miss the point of Luke's intent. It is not about tongues; it is about this angry man named Saul, who persecuted the church, coming to a dramatic conversion. Luke pits Saul against Christians and the Christ they serve only to shock us with the amazing fact that Saul becomes a convert to the faith he once tried to destroy!

It is interesting to note that Luke was talking about the great apostle Paul in this passage. Luke had an exemplary opportunity to establish a paradigm if this was what he intended to do. Who better to use by way of example than the apostle Paul in describing "how it is to be done"? Luke did not write chapter nine without knowing about the information in chapter twenty-eight, and all the information between chapters nine and twenty-eight. Luke intimately knew who Paul was, and how Paul had set himself up as an example to be followed (2 Thessalonians 3:7-9). Yet, Luke is not the least bit interested in establishing a paradigm for tongues as the initial, physical evidence of the baptism in the Holy Spirit by using Paul as his example.

Luke does, however, establish a *salvific paradigm* of the extent to which God's grace travels to reach even the worst enemies of the Cross. Reflecting on this very truth, Paul later says, "Here is a trustworthy saying that deserves full acceptance: Christ Jesus came into the world to save sinners—of whom I am the worst" (1 Timothy 1:15). The paradigm that Luke establishes in his account of the conversion/baptism of the Holy Spirit in the life of Saul is that the worst sinners can be saved through the mighty power of God. Can anyone reading this account miss Luke's true emphasis here?

At this point I am only attempting to lead the reader to the obvious conclusion that Luke does not intend to establish tongues-as-evidence as a doctrine or as a paradigm. If Luke is trying to establish that "tongues is the initial, physical evidence of the baptism in the Holy Spirit," and if he is attempting to establish this idea as a doctrine or as a paradigm for all Christians, then he is miserably failing at his task.

However, Luke is not a substandard communicator. If Scripture is allowed to "speak for itself" without one's control beliefs being pressed upon it, it becomes obvious that Luke's intent is to establish the soteriological nature of the early church in conjunction with the preaching of the gospel and the infilling of the Holy Spirit. Luke has *clearly* demonstrated this theme so far, and he does a wonderful job of showing his readers that this Saul who came to persecute believers has himself come to a cataclysmic salvation in Jesus Christ. This is communication *par excellence*. Luke is clearly communicating *what it is that he wants to communicate*, and tongues as the initial, physical evidence of the baptism in the Holy Spirit is not it. Salvation is.

The Church Throughout Judea Grew in Number
Acts 9:31

> Then the church throughout Judea, Galilee and Samaria enjoyed a time of peace. It was strengthened; and encouraged by the Holy Spirit, it grew in numbers, living in the fear of the Lord.

The church grew in number. Luke's emphasis continues to be all about salvation.

Turned to the Lord
Acts 9:35

> All those who lived in Lydda and Sharon saw him and turned to the Lord.

Here Luke stays true to his theme and says that people "turned to the Lord." Note that speaking in tongues is not mentioned.

Speaking in Tongues and Praising God
Acts 10:44-48

> While Peter was still speaking these words,

the Holy Spirit came on all who heard the message. The circumcised believers who had come with Peter were astonished that the gift of the Holy Spirit had been poured out even on the Gentiles. For they heard them speaking in tongues and praising God. Then Peter said, "Can anyone keep these people from being baptized with water? They have received the Holy Spirit just as we have." So he ordered that they be baptized in the name of Jesus Christ. Then they asked Peter to stay with them for a few days.

This is only the second passage in Acts that explicitly states that Christians spoke in tongues. Cornelius and his household received the Holy Spirit as Peter preached to them (Acts 10:44-46). The first physical evidence that they had received the Holy Spirit was that they spoke in tongues (10:46).

Peter was so convinced that speaking in tongues was the evidence that the Holy Spirit had filled these Gentile believers that he challenged: "Can anyone keep these people from being baptized with water? They have received the Holy Spirit just as we have" (10:47). Clearly, in the *specific* case of the "Cornelius experience," Peter recognized that these Gentiles had received the Holy Spirit because he saw and heard them speaking in tongues.

In Peter's thinking, speaking in tongues was connected with the baptism in the Spirit (a salvation experience). If not, he would not have accepted the Cornelius experience of speaking in tongues as the undeniable evidence that Cornelius (and the other

Gentiles present) had received the "gift of the Father" (Acts 1:4). Peter later explained that Cornelius and his household had received the Spirit (Acts 10:44-46) in these words, "As I began to speak, the Holy Spirit came on them as he had come on us at the beginning" (Acts 11:15; 15:8).

But why did Peter have to give an explanation? The context indicates that the Jewish Christians were not pleased with Peter's actions of having entered into a Gentile's home and having eaten with them: "So when Peter went up to Jerusalem, the circumcised believers criticized him and said, 'You went into the house of uncircumcised men and ate with them'" (Acts 11:2-3). Many of the Jewish Christians firmly believed that there was no change in the way they were to view Gentiles. They were considered unworthy of the salvation of God, and a Jew (be he a Christian or not) would be defiled by entering into their homes or by eating with them. To defend his actions and to show that God was accepting repentant Gentiles, Peter tells them that God had sent him to Cornelius' home and that:

> As I began to speak, the Holy Spirit came on them as he had on us at the beginning. . . . So if God gave them the same gift as He gave us, who believed in the Lord Jesus Christ, who was I to think that I could oppose God (Acts 11:15, 17)?

When the Jewish Christians heard that God had given them the gift of the Holy Spirit, which was evidenced by their speaking in tongues, they said, "So then, God has granted even the Gentiles repentance unto life" (Acts

11:18).

Certainly, the Gentiles' speaking in tongues was the initial, physical evidence that they had been baptized in the Holy Spirit, but actually it went further than that. For the Jewish Christians, the speaking in tongues by the Gentiles was *evidence of their salvation*. Notice that after Peter explains to them what transpired, the Jewish Christians do not say, "So then, God has granted even the Gentiles the baptism in the Holy Spirit." Rather, they say, "So then, God has granted even the Gentiles *repentance unto life*" (emphasis added, Acts 11:18). Luke undeniably shows this as a *soteriological issue*. The primary conclusion that the Jewish Christians reached due to this experience of tongues-speaking was a *soteriological conclusion*, not a pneumatological one. The pneumatological naturally follows, but it is secondary. Salvation is primary and is Luke's emphasis.

The tongues speaking was evidence to them (and only within this historical, singular context) that the Gentiles were allowed "repentance unto life." Does this mean then if one does not speak in tongues that he is not saved? Absolutely not. The tongues-speaking was a sign for the Jews not for the Gentiles. The Jews needed some *recognizable evidence* that God had accepted the Gentiles, and this is what the Lord chose to provide.

But, once the Jews recognized the fact that God had "granted even the Gentiles repentance unto life" (Acts 11:18), they did not need to see that evidence again. That Gentiles could be saved was then, for them, an established fact. Undoubtedly, other Gentiles later also spoke in tongues, but the Jews no longer needed an evidential sign to know that God was bringing the Gentiles into His kingdom.

Let's review our guiding question: "What importance does Luke give to tongues as evidence of the baptism in the Holy Spirit?" Even in this very charismatic passage, the importance that Luke gives to *tongues as evidence* is directed to the issue of salvation and to the fact that the Jews could see that God had "granted even the Gentiles repentance unto life." Luke's theme is consistently—and powerfully—soteriological.

Evidence Is Not Contingency

It also should be noted that evidence is not the same thing as contingency. In other words, the Gentiles speaking in tongues may have been the evidence to the Jewish Christians that the Gentiles were saved, but their salvation was *not contingent* upon the evidence of speaking in tongues. The sound of an airplane flying overhead may be an evidence to a person below that the plane is flying overhead, but the plane's flight overhead is not dependent upon that person hearing it. Likewise, their speaking in tongues was not what saved the Gentiles, but it was the initial (first), physical (outward) evidence (not contingency) *to the Jewish Christians* that God was granting salvation to the Gentiles. Seen in this soteriological light, this passage may say more about the Jewish Christians than it does about tongues as evidence of the baptism in the Holy Spirit. It is important to see the full context of the Cornelius experience.

> At Caesarea there was a man named Cornelius, a centurion in what was known as the Italian Regiment. He and all his family were devout and God-fearing; he gave generously to those in need and prayed to God regularly. One day at about three in the afternoon he had a vision. He distinctly saw an angel of God, who came to him and said, "Cornelius!" Cornelius stared at him in fear. "What is it, Lord?" he asked. The angel answered, "Your prayers and gifts to the poor have come up as a memorial offering before God. Now send men to Joppa to bring back a man named Simon who is called Peter. He is staying with Simon the tanner, whose house is by the sea." When the angel who spoke to him had gone, Cornelius called two of his servants and a devout soldier who was one of his attendants. He told them everything that had happened and sent them to Joppa (Acts 10:1-8).

Cornelius sends two of his servants and one of his attendants to Joppa to fetch Peter, the Jew. But before these men arrive at the house where Peter is staying, God works on Peter's heart. The passage goes on to say:

> About noon the following day as they were on their journey and approaching the city, Peter went up on the roof to pray. He became hungry and wanted something to eat, and while the meal was being prepared, he fell into a trance. He saw heaven opened and something like a large sheet being let down to earth by its four corners. It contained all kinds of four-footed animals, as well as reptiles of the earth and birds of the air. Then

> a voice told him, "Get up, Peter. Kill and eat." "Surely not, Lord!" Peter replied. "I have never eaten anything impure or unclean." The voice spoke to him a second time, "Do not call anything impure that God has made clean." This happened three times, and immediately the sheet was taken back to heaven (Acts 10:9-16).

So while the servants are on their way to seek Peter, God is preparing Peter's heart. God says to Peter, "Do not call anything impure that God has made clean." And, this happens not just one time, but for emphatic effect, it happens three times. The passage continues:

> While Peter was wondering about the meaning of the vision, the men sent by Cornelius found out where Simon's house was and stopped at the gate. They called out, asking if Simon who was known as Peter was staying there. While Peter was still thinking about the vision, the Spirit said to him, "Simon, three men are looking for you. So get up and go downstairs. Do not hesitate to go with them, for I have sent them" (Acts 10:17-20).

Note how emphatic the Holy Spirit is being with Peter. First he gives him a vision that makes crystal clear that God has now made clean some things that were formerly impure. Then, while Peter is wondering about the meaning of the vision, the Gentile servants arrive asking for him. Not only that, but the Holy Spirit talks to Peter at the same time and says that the men who are asking for him are sent by God and that he should not hesitate to go with them. Why would he have been hesitant to eat unclean food or travel with Gentiles? First, not all foods were kosher. Next, the Jews did not associate with Gentiles. In fact, it was against their law! The passage goes on:

> Peter went down and said to the men, "I'm the one you're looking for. Why have you come?" The men replied, "We have come from Cornelius the centurion. He is a righteous and God-fearing man, who is respected by all the Jewish people. A holy angel told him to have you come to his house so that he could hear what you have to say." Then Peter invited the men into the house to be his guests. The next day Peter started out with them, and some of the brothers from Joppa went along. The following day he arrived in Caesarea. Cornelius was expecting them and had called together his relatives and close friends. As Peter entered the house, Cornelius met him and fell at his feet in reverence. But Peter made him get up. "Stand up," he said, "I am only a man myself." Talking with him, Peter went inside and found a large gathering of people. He said to them: "You are well aware that it is against our law for a Jew to associate with a Gentile or visit him. But God has shown me that I should not call any man impure or unclean (Acts 10:21-28).

To make all of this context perfectly clear, Luke records these words of Peter: "You are well aware that it is against our law for a Jew to associate with a Gentile or visit him. But God has shown me that I should not call any man impure or unclean." The vision has made its impact upon Peter. The implication of the vision is becoming clear to him. God is doing something with the Gentiles. Peter goes on:

> So when I was sent for, I came without raising any objection. May I ask why you sent for me?" Cornelius answered: "Four days ago I was in my house praying at this hour, at three in the afternoon. Suddenly a man in shining clothes stood before me and said, 'Cornelius, God has heard your prayer and remembered your gifts to the poor. Send to Joppa for Simon who is called Peter. He is a guest in the home of Simon the tanner, who lives by the sea.' So I sent for you immediately, and it was good of you to come. Now we are all here in the presence of God to listen to everything the Lord has commanded you to tell us." Then Peter began to speak: "I now realize how true it is that God does not show favoritism but accepts men from every nation who fear him and do what is right" (Acts 10:29-35).

This then is the context of the "Cornelius experience," and it is a clear one: Salvation for the Gentiles. Previously the Jews did not accept the Gentiles; in fact, it was against their law to even associate with them. What then must God do to show the Jews that he is going to save the Gentiles too? What evidence will he provide for these exclusive Jews? Obviously he needs to use something visible so their senses can comprehend it. It also must be something unmistakably connected to him and to them so that their minds cannot rationally reject it.

Peter begins to preach the gospel to these Gentiles.

He told of Christ's crucifixion, his resurrection, and that "everyone who believes in him receives forgiveness of sins through his name" (Acts 10:36-43). This is a soteriological context. And while he is telling them this, God demonstrates with an outward visible sign that these Gentiles have just had their sins forgiven through Jesus Christ (a soteriological outcome). And, how does he demonstrate this to these Jews? He gives them a visible phenomenon which they could spiritually identify with, speaking in tongues. In fact, the Jewish believers with Peter were *astonished* that the gift of the Holy Spirit had been poured out even on the Gentiles. Then, after God has clearly demonstrated that he has saved these Gentiles, Peter says, "Can anyone keep these people from being baptized with water? They have received the Holy Spirit just as we have" (Acts 10:47).

How can it be proven that the primary purpose for speaking in tongues in this single instance is to provide evidence to the Jews of the Gentiles' salvation? Because, Luke records that this is the very argument that Peter took to the Jewish Christians (Acts 15:8)! So, once again, Luke further demonstrates the soteriological thread line that has been running throughout the book of Acts.

Therefore, in the "Cornelius context" speaking in tongues was not just the initial, physical evidence of the baptism in the Holy Spirit; it was in fact the initial, physical evidence of salvation that convinced an exclusive group of Jewish Christians that God was now accepting the Gentiles. However, it should be pointed out that this singular situation certainly does not establish a methodological paradigm.

Some are so afraid to allow any "tongues-as-an-evidence ground," that they will do all sorts of semantic and hermeneutical gymnastics to keep from saying that tongues in the "Cornelius context" were the initial, physical evidence of either the baptism in the Holy Spirit or of salvation. However, this fear is unnecessary. A unique or even occasional occurrence does not establish a paradigm. What may be a normal experience for some Christians is not necessarily a norm for all Christians. The manifestation of tongues in the "Cornelius context" is descriptive, not prescriptive. So, while tongues is a clear evidence to Peter, and to the other Jewish Christians, that God had "granted even the Gentiles repentance unto life" (Acts 11:18), this does not establish a normal pattern to be imposed upon all Christians for all time. Once it had been established that God accepts both Jews and Gentiles, no further initial, outward salvific evidence is necessary.

Luke's intent is consistently soteriological. Also, it should be pointed out that this particular experience of Spirit baptism and tongues does not appear to be a subsequent and second work of grace; it appears to be simultaneous with salvation.

Peter Defends His Actions
Acts 11:1-18

> The apostles and the brothers throughout Judea heard that the Gentiles also had received the word of God. So when Peter went up to Jerusalem, the circumcised believers criticized him and said, "You went into the

house of uncircumcised men and ate with them." Peter began and explained everything to them precisely as it had happened: "I was in the city of Joppa praying, and in a trance I saw a vision. I saw something like a large sheet being let down from heaven by its four corners, and it came down to where I was. I looked into it and saw four-footed animals of the earth, wild beasts, reptiles, and birds of the air. Then I heard a voice telling me, 'Get up, Peter. Kill and eat.' "I replied, 'Surely not, Lord! Nothing impure or unclean has ever entered my mouth.' "The voice spoke from heaven a second time, 'Do not call anything impure that God has made clean.' This happened three times, and then it was all pulled up to heaven again. "Right then three men who had been sent to me from Caesarea stopped at the house where I was staying. The Spirit told me to have no hesitation about going with them. These six brothers also went with me, and we entered the man's house. He told us how he had seen an angel appear in his house and say, 'Send to Joppa for Simon who is called Peter. He will bring you a message through which you and all your household will be saved.' "As I began to speak, the Holy Spirit came on them as he had come on us at the beginning. Then I remembered what the Lord had said: 'John baptized with water, but you will be baptized with the Holy Spirit.' So if God gave them the same gift as he gave us, who believed in the Lord Jesus Christ, who was I to think that I could oppose God?" When they heard this, they had no further objections and praised God, saying, "So then, God has granted even the Gentiles repentance unto life."

Peter here has to defend his actions of entering into the home of Gentiles and eating with them. See the information about this event in the material above under Acts 10:44.

People Believed and Turned to the Lord
Acts 11:21

> The Lord's hand was with them, and a great number of people believed and turned to the Lord.

"A great number of people believed and turned to the Lord." Luke mentions salvation, but not tongues. His emphasis is soteriological, not tongues as an evidence of the baptism in the Holy Spirit.

Paul Filled with the Holy Spirit
Acts 13:9-10

> Then Saul, who was also called Paul, filled with the Holy Spirit, looked straight at Elymas and said, "You are a child of the devil and an enemy of everything that is right! You are full of all kinds of deceit and trickery. Will you never stop perverting the right ways of the Lord?"

Paul was filled with the Holy Spirit and pronounced blindness upon Elymas. Here, Luke says that Paul was "filled with the Holy Spirit." Speaking in tongues is not mentioned here, but of course it wouldn't be. This account is not speaking of the same thing that transpired on the day of Pentecost nor that transpires when one is newly saved and filled with the Holy Spirit. This text will be discussed below. It is mentioned here only because the term "filled with the Holy Spirit" is used.

The Proconsul Believed
Acts 13:12

> When the proconsul saw what had happened, he believed, for he was amazed at the teaching about the Lord.

In this passage, Luke says that the proconsul believed. Speaking in tongues is not mentioned. Luke's intent? Soteriological.

Appointed for Eternal Life
Acts 13:48

> When the Gentiles heard this, they were glad and honored the word of the Lord; and all who were appointed for eternal life believed.

In this passage Luke says that some Gentiles believed. Speaking in tongues is not mentioned. One might ask why the Gentiles in chapter ten (the "Cornelius context") spoke in tongues and these Gentiles did not, or at least why Luke does not record that they did. The answer must emerge from Luke's intent. In chapter ten Luke established that God accepts repentant Gentiles. Now, all that is necessary is that they put their faith in Christ; no further outward signs are necessary to prove to the Jews that God accepts these Gentile converts. By now, they already know this. Luke's intent continues to be soteriological.

Jews and Gentiles Believed
Acts 14:1
> At Iconium Paul and Barnabas went as usual into the Jewish synagogue. There they spoke so effectively that a great number of Jews and Gentiles believed.

In this passage, Luke says that a great number of Jews and Gentiles believed. Speaking in tongues is not mentioned. Luke's intent? Soteriological.

A Large Number of Disciples
Acts 14:21-22
> They preached the good news in that city and won a large number of disciples. Then they returned to Lystra, Iconium and Antioch, strengthening the disciples and encouraging them to remain true to the faith. "We must go through many hardships to enter the kingdom of God," they said.

In this passage, Luke says that a large number of people became disciples. Speaking in tongues is not mentioned. Luke continues his soteriological theme.

He Purified Their Hearts by Faith
Acts 15:4-9
> When they came to Jerusalem, they were welcomed by the church and the apostles and elders, to whom they reported everything God had done through them. Then some of the believers who belonged to the party of the Pharisees stood up and said, "The Gentiles

> must be circumcised and required to obey the law of Moses." The apostles and elders met to consider this question. After much discussion, Peter got up and addressed them: "Brothers, you know that some time ago God made a choice among you that the Gentiles might hear from my lips the message of the gospel and believe. God, who knows the heart, showed that he accepted them by giving the Holy Spirit to them, just as he did to us. He made no distinction between us and them, for he purified their hearts by faith.

Peter again argues that Gentiles are able to be saved apart from the law. He does this by pointing out that God gave them the Holy Spirit (cf., Acts 10:44). Since the Gentiles can be *saved* apart from the law, they should not have the law imposed upon them. Luke's intent? Soteriological.

The Churches Grew Daily in Number
Acts 16:5
> So the churches were strengthened in the faith and grew daily in numbers.

In this passage, Luke says that the church "grew daily in numbers." Speaking in tongues is not mentioned even though people were daily coming to faith in Jesus Christ. Luke's intent? Soteriological.

The Lord Opened Her Heart
Acts 16:14-15
> One of those listening was a woman named Lydia, a dealer in purple cloth from the city of Thyatira, who was a worshiper of God. The Lord opened her heart to respond to Paul's message. When she and the members of her household were baptized, she invited us to her home. "If you consider me a believer in the Lord," she said, "come and stay at my house." And she persuaded us.

Lydia and the members of her household are saved and baptized, but again Luke is silent about the issue of speaking in tongues. His intent is soteriological.

He and All His Family Were Baptized
Acts 16:29-34
> The jailer called for lights, rushed in and fell trembling before Paul and Silas. He then brought them out and asked, "Sirs, what must I do to be saved?" They replied, "Believe in the Lord Jesus, and you will be saved—you and your household." Then they spoke the word of the Lord to him and to all the others in his house. At that hour of the night the jailer took them and washed their wounds; then immediately he and all his family were baptized. The jailer brought them into his house and set a meal before them; he was filled with joy because he had come to believe in God—he and his whole family.

Luke records the account of the Philippian jailer and the members of his household getting saved and being baptized, but, again, he does not mention speaking in tongues. His intent continues to be soteriological in nature. Luke is *not emphasizing* tongues.

It behooves Christians to follow his leading since he was led by the Holy Spirit to record the events *as he did*. Christians must not major on the minors, and when we place a greater emphasis upon *occasional* aspects of the overall package of salvation than Luke or the Holy Spirit does, then we are out of balance.

Some of the Jews Were Persuaded
Acts 17:4

> Some of the Jews were persuaded and joined Paul and Silas, as did a large number of God-fearing Greeks and not a few prominent women.

In this passage, Luke says that a great number of Gentiles, some Jews, and some "prominent women" believed. Again, he makes no mention of tongues. He does not deviate from his soteriological intent, nor does he deviate from his lack of mentioning tongues.

Many of the Jews Believed
Acts 17:12

> Many of the Jews believed, as did also a number of prominent Greek women and many Greek men.

In this passage, Luke says that a great number of Gentiles, Jews, and women believed. Again there is no mention of speaking in tongues. Luke's intent continues to be soteriological in nature.

A Few Men Believed
Acts 17:34
> A few men became followers of Paul and believed. Among them was Dionysius, a member of the Areopagus, also a woman named Damaris, and a number of others.

Luke says that a few people believed. He even details the names of some of them. But he makes no mention of tongues. His intent remains strongly soteriological.

Many of the Corinthians Believed
Acts 18:8
> Crispus, the synagogue ruler, and his entire household believed in the Lord; and many of the Corinthians who heard him believed and were baptized.

In the context of this passage, Paul is in Corinth. This is the city in which the infamous "super spiritual" Corinthians resided. The Corinthians were those to whom Paul wrote and whom he corrected on matters of church conduct. Not the least of the problems in Corinth was the issue of an imbalance with regard to speaking in tongues (see 1 Corinthians 14:6-28). Acts 18 gives the account of when it all began.

One might think that Luke would have made a point of mentioning tongues with regard to the beginnings of the church that was later so given to tongues in its gatherings. Yet all Luke says is that "Crispus, the synagogue ruler, and his entire household believed in the Lord; and many of the Corinthians who heard him believed and were baptized" (v. 8). It is well known that many in Corinth spoke in tongues. Yet, *apparently*, Luke did not consider tongues to be of outstanding significance. It is noteworthy that Acts 18:11 says that Paul "stayed for a year and a half, teaching them the word of God." And still Luke does not mention tongues. His intent continues to be consistently soteriological.

They Spoke in Tongues and Prophesied
Acts 19:6

> When Paul placed his hands on them, the Holy Spirit came on them, and they spoke in tongues and prophesied.

Here is an account of some disciples in Ephesus. Paul asks them, "Did you receive the Holy Spirit when you believed?" Luke does not explain what prompted Paul to ask this question. Apparently after talking to them for a while, he discerned something was lacking in them, so he asked if they had received the Holy Spirit. Notice what appears to be Paul's surprise when they respond by saying, "No, we have not even heard that there is a Holy Spirit" (v. 2b). In the next verse, Paul says, "Then what baptism did you receive?" The implication is obvious. If they do not have the Holy Spirit, they obviously did not receive Christian baptism. John's baptism pointed to the Messiah and says that one is to get ready to enter into the messianic kingdom. There is more for these "disciples." There is the entering into the kingdom of God, and it is the Holy Spirit who ushers them into this kingdom (1 Corinthians 12:13). If they have not received the Holy Spirit, they have not entered into the kingdom of God.

This is only the third (and final) occasion in which Luke identifies those who received the Holy Spirit as having spoken in tongues. "When Paul placed his hands on them, the Holy Spirit came on them, and they spoke in tongues and prophesied" (Acts 19:6). Note that the text also just as clearly states that they prophesied.

Some Classical Pentecostals argue that prophecy is not as important an evidence as tongues in this context. They argue that only speaking in tongues is the "evidence" of the baptism in the Holy Spirit. But why elevate tongues over prophecy in this way? There is no exegetical reason to do so. It is done simply because it fits into their preconceived theological position. If we are going to be evenhanded with the text, we cannot simply subjugate prophecy to tongues in this passage. The plain fact of Scripture is this: If speaking in tongues in this passage is "evidential," then so too is prophecy. This makes this passage *unique* since there are two evidences and not just one, and it also makes this passage *different from* the other two passages in which people spoke in tongues.

So, of the three texts in which people explicitly spoke in tongues, Acts 2 says that they spoke in tongues as part of the initial outpouring of the Holy Spirit, Acts 10 indicates that they spoke in tongues as a sign to the Jews that God was accepting the Gentiles into the kingdom of

God, and here in Acts 19, they not only spoke in tongues but they prophesied as well. The obvious inconsistency of this outward manifestation in these three (and only three!) accounts is a clear indication that Luke was not developing a theology of "tongues-as-evidence." These three *inconsistent* occasions simply do not establish a paradigm.

Who Are You Lord?
Acts 22:6-16

> About noon as I came near Damascus, suddenly a bright light from heaven flashed around me. I fell to the ground and heard a voice say to me, 'Saul! Saul! Why do you persecute me?' " 'Who are you, Lord?' I asked. 'I am Jesus of Nazareth, whom you are persecuting,' he replied. My companions saw the light, but they did not understand the voice of him who was speaking to me. "'What shall I do, Lord?' I asked. 'Get up,' the Lord said, 'and go into Damascus. There you will be told all that you have been assigned to do.' My companions led me by the hand into Damascus, because the brilliance of the light had blinded me. "A man named Ananias came to see me. He was a devout observer of the law and highly respected by all the Jews living there. He stood beside me and said, 'Brother Saul, receive your sight!' And at that very moment I was able to see him. "Then he said: 'The God of our fathers has chosen you to know his will and to see the Righteous One and to hear words from his mouth. You will be his witness to all men of what you have seen and heard. And now what are you

waiting for? Get up, be baptized and wash your sins away, calling on his name.'

There is a stark contrast between the recounting of the Holy Spirit baptism by some present-day Classical Pentecostals and the apostle's account of his own experience. Having been in Pentecostal circles for more than half of my lifetime, I have heard many accounts of Classical Pentecostals who recounted in detail their experience of speaking in tongues on the occasions of—what they claim was—the baptism in the Holy Spirit. Never once was such an account missing the detail that they had "spoken in other tongues." In fact, had that detail been missing, they would not have been testifying to their "baptism in the Holy Spirit." Yet, interestingly, in this passage (Acts 22:6-16) Paul recounts his conversion/baptism in the Holy Spirit experience, but he does not mention speaking in tongues.

It is interesting to note how very detailed he was in his recounting of his conversion/baptism in the Holy Spirit experience. He mentions the time of day, "about noon"; the location, "near Damascus"; a "bright light"; his response, "I fell to the ground"; what he heard, "a voice say to me, 'Saul! Saul! Why do you persecute me?'" His response, "Who are you, Lord?" The voice's response, "I am Jesus of Nazareth." He tells of the details of who saw the light, "My companions," but he is careful to point out that "they did not understand the voice." He submits to the voice, "What shall I do, Lord?" He is then very careful to tell his listeners what exactly the Lord tells him to do, "Get up and go into Damascus," and there are yet more details. He tells how he had to be "led by the hand into Damascus" because he had become blinded by the light. Next, he mentions Ananias by name. He details how Ananias was a devout observer of the law and highly respected by all the Jews. He details how Ananias "stood beside" him, and he gives Ananias's very words. Paul then says that it was at that "very moment" that he was able to see. Paul goes on to detail what more Ananias said to him, and that Paul was to be (a witness) for the Lord. And, he even mentions that Ananias seems to chide him with the words, "And now what are you waiting for? Get up, be baptized and wash your sins away, calling on his name."

The itemization that Paul gives is painstakingly detailed, almost to the point of being boring. Yet, in this most important, itemized, detailed recounting of his conversion/Holy-Spirit-baptism experience, he does *not* mention speaking in tongues. In fact, he does not even mention the baptism in the Holy Spirit *per se*. The great "Pentecostal Paul" who spoke in tongues more than *all* of the Corinthians (1 Corinthians 14:18) does not mention his baptism in the Holy Spirit with the initial, physical evidence of speaking in other tongues! Certainly in some Classical Pentecostal circles Paul would have been rebuked and corrected for passing over such a *significant* point as this.

Once again, the basic question comes to the surface: *Just how important can this whole issue be when Paul himself does not even mention it in his itemized, detailed recounting of his own conversion/Holy-Spirit-baptism experience?* This question is especially important when one recognizes that Classical Pentecostals *insist* that Paul *did speak in tongues at the time of his conversion/Spirit baptism.*[5] But how, one might ask, can we be sure he spoke in tongues at that time? Horton asserts this "sureness" without providing evidence that it is so. His argument that it can be inferred from the fact that the 120 on the day of Pentecost did and therefore others who receive the baptism in the Spirit likewise do is unconvincing.

Concluding Remarks

I have been arguing that the authorial intent, i.e., Luke's intent, throughout the book of Acts is *soteriological.* An honest evaluation of the various passages in Acts that speak of the baptism (or filling) in (or with) the Holy Spirit and salvation lead me to conclude that *Luke's intent* was clearly and predominantly soteriological. However, this fact in and of itself is not proof that speaking in tongues is not the initial, physical evidence of the baptism in the Holy Spirit. What it does prove, however, is that many Christians in the Classical Pentecostal tradition have majored on a minor and have become out of balance on this point.

If Luke mentions the outward manifestation of tongues on only three of twenty-six soteriological occasions, with the number of people demonstrating this outward manifestation to be around 150 out of well over three thousand people, then the obvious question must follow, *How important could it have possibly been to Luke?* And, if the apostle Paul does not even mention his "tongues experience" when recounting his own conversion/Holy-Spirit-baptism experience, once again the obvious question is, *How important could it have possibly been to Paul?*

Obviously it was not as important to either Luke or Paul as was the salvation of people. Rather than saying that "tongues is the initial, physical evidence of the baptism in the Holy Spirit," it actually appears that all that can be legitimately said about the issue of "evidence" with regard to *speaking in tongues* as depicted by Luke is that *speaking in tongues* was (1) *occasional* and (2) the outward *physical* evidence to some of the *Christian Jews* within the historical context of the book of Acts that outsiders had received the Holy Spirit, and thus, *more to the point*, salvation—"So then, God has granted even the Gentiles repentance unto life" (Acts 11:18).

End Notes

¹ Gordon D. Fee, *Gospel and Spirit: Issues in New Testament Hermeneutics* (Peabody, MA.: Hendrickson Publishers, Inc., 1991), p. 43. There may be exceptions with regard to prophecies about future events that were to transpire after the time of the author's writing.

² Stanley M. Horton, *The Book of Acts* (Springfield, MO.: Gospel Publishing House, 1981), p. 47.

³ Ibid.

⁴ Ibid., p. 105.

⁵ Ibid., p. 119.

Chapter 6

Argument # 2: Three Times out of Five? Does This Establish a Paradigm?

Inductive and Deductive Reasoning

Some Classical Pentecostals contend that three explicit statements of tongues-speaking out of a total of five passages in which the "baptism in the Holy Spirit" is mentioned is enough evidence to provide a paradigm. Also, in the other two (of the five), it appears that the idea that the people spoke in tongues is implied. This, they argue, is a good case of deductive reasoning.

However, one should ask "What of the thousands of other converts of whom Luke says nothing about them speaking in tongues?" Was it that they were saved but not filled with the Spirit? This is clearly a non-biblical notion. Yet, many Classical Pentecostals argue that if one has not spoken in tongues, he simply has not been baptized in the Holy Spirit. If one allows the premise to be, "When one is baptized in the Holy Spirit, he will, of necessity, speak in other tongues," then one must logically conclude that if one does not speak in tongues, he simply has not been baptized in the Holy Spirit. In syllogistic style, the Classical Pentecostal's argument looks like this:

—The Baptism in the Holy Spirit is always evidenced by speaking in tongues.

—Some Christians do not speak in tongues.

—Therefore, some Christians have not been baptized in the Holy Spirit.

However, it is not at all certain that the premise is correct. It will be shown, rather, that the premise the Classical Pentecostal begins with is flawed.

I agree with Gordon Fee on this issue. The baptism of the Holy Spirit is the eschatological "door" through which people travel to enter into the age to come, the messianic age. Thus, if they are saved, they are, as a matter of course, baptized in the Holy Spirit. In syllogistic style, this argument looks like this:

—The Baptism in the Holy Spirit is the eschatological "door" to the age to come.

—All Christians are heading to that age to come.

—Therefore, all Christians have been baptized in the Holy Spirit.

If these thousands of people (throughout the book of Acts) were being saved and yet not filled with the Holy Spirit and none of the New Testament writers discussed this nor decried it, then it must be asked, "Why did not the biblical writers make an issue out of this lack of Holy Spirit baptism?" If Classical Pentecostals are right about the *significance of speaking in tongues*, then one would expect one of two things in the biblical record: (a) the constant and thorough demonstration of this gift throughout the pages of the New Testament (starting with the book of Acts), or, since this constant and thorough demonstration is not seen throughout the pages of the New Testament, one should expect to see (b) the didactic correction by New Testament writers who then instruct people to seek the highly desirable gift of the baptism in the Holy Spirit *with the evidence of speaking in tongues*. But, neither of these two things is seen in the pages of New Testament writ.

Throughout the book of Acts, many were *saved* and *filled* with the Holy Spirit, but even so, Luke does not record that they spoke in tongues. Why did he not record this? The most simple answer and the one which best fits with the scriptural evidence is that *it was not his intent to do so*. Had it been, he surely would have. Luke was not trying to teach a theological point about "baptism in the Holy Spirit and speaking in tongues." He was simply reporting on the soteriological nature of the events and the consequent charismatic effects, in that order and with that emphasis.

Luke clearly demonstrates from a few examples that when Jews and Gentiles came into the Messianic kingdom, they were filled with the Holy Spirit. On only three occasions, the outward, initial, physical evidence was that these converts spoke in tongues by the power of the Holy Spirit. However, since Luke does not make "tongues as evidence" a primary emphasis, neither should we. Luke is far more concerned with the fact that people (1) got saved through their repentance and belief in Jesus Christ, (2) entered into Christ's kingdom, and (3) were indwelt by the Holy Spirit. In Luke's own record, speaking in tongues is incidental and occasional, not requisite and constant.

Some non-Pentecostal Christians have charged Classical Pentecostals with the logical fallacy of hasty generalization through careless inductive reasoning. However, Classical Pentecostals have always thought that their argument was a deductive one. Classical Pentecostals have long argued that the divine paradigm is that speaking in tongues is the initial, physical evidence of the baptism in the Holy Spirit. After all, when there is a total of *five* situations (as Classical Pentecostals teach), and three of the five state beyond a doubt that speaking in tongues was the outward manifestation of the infilling of the Holy Spirit, and of the remaining two a good case can be built that one of them indicates that tongues were once again the outward manifestation of the Spirit infilling, then the argument is a strongly deductive one. However, and this is really the point, was it three out of five?

Inductive and Deductive Explained

Both inductive and deductive reasoning may be used to discover truth, but deductive reasoning is far more conclusive than inductive reasoning. Inductive reasoning moves from the particular to the general, and if not careful one can reach a hasty generalization. A hasty generalization is when the size of the sample is too small to support the conclusion.

Inductive reasoning can be depicted as a triangle with the base at the bottom and the point at the top, i.e., ▲. Inductive reasoning starts at that top point with limited information and then draws a general conclusion at the bottom. The weakness of inductive reasoning is that one does not have enough evidence (at the top) to be sure of the (wide-based) conclusion.

Deductive reasoning, however, would invert the triangle, i.e.,▼. This represents that the information line would be broader, and the deductive argument's conclusion actually follows from the reasoning presented.

In inductive reasoning, the conclusion might not logically follow because one is attempting to make a generalized statement on the basis of only a few examples. For example, let's say that you have met three men named John. Now, let's say that all three men were crooks. Shall you then conclude that all men named John are crooks? Since there are millions of men named John, making a conclusion about all of them from such a small number is simply a hasty generalization, i.e., not supported by the size of the sample.

Classical Pentecostals contend that there are three out of five situations in which Scripture explicitly states that people spoke in tongues. Of the remaining two, it can be adequately argued that those in question spoke in tongues. Thus, says the Classical Pentecostal, the weight of the evidence is for all to speak in tongues when they are baptized in the Holy Spirit. It is God's desire that everyone follow this *three-out-of-five paradigm.*

If this is accurate, that there are three of five occasions in which people spoke in tongues, then it would be considered deductive reasoning and highly probable, but still not absolute. However, were there only five instances in which people received the infilling of the Holy Spirit? Listed below are the five occasions that Classical Pentecostals point to for their evidence.

The First Occasion: The Day of Pentecost
Acts 2:4

In Acts the second chapter, the 120 disciples "were all filled with the Holy Spirit and began to speak with other tongues, as the Spirit gave them utterance" (Acts 2:4). This incident hardly needs a thorough discussion. It is so clear that one can say that tongues was an accompaniment (a sign) of the baptism in the Holy Spirit on this *particular* occasion. All must agree that there is no contest to this conclusion. For Scripture says that the disciples "were all filled with the Holy Spirit and began to speak with other tongues, as the Spirit gave them utterance." Also, note that *all 120* were filled and spoke with tongues.

The Second Occasion: The Samaritan Experience
Acts 8:14-17

Many *infer* that speaking in tongues is the initial, physical evidence of the baptism in the Holy Spirit from this passage. One point must be made. The baptism in the Holy Spirit that came to the Samaritans was a dynamic and sudden experience. The biblical account says, "Then they laid their hands on them, and they received the Holy Ghost" (Acts 8:17). This was not a gradual experience, nor does it depict a baptism in the Spirit that was only spiritual (i.e., inward) and not visible. How did they know that these Samaritan disciples *received* the Holy Spirit? By circumstantial evidence, many Pentecostals conclude that they literally *saw and heard* something transpire which convinced them.

> And when Simon saw that through laying on of the apostles' hands the Holy Ghost was given, he offered them money, saying, "Give me also this power, that on whomsoever I lay hands, he may receive the Holy Ghost" (emphasis added, Acts 8:18-19).

There undoubtedly was an outward accompaniment (evidence) of the reception of the Spirit. But what was this visible outward accompaniment? Remember also that Philip had already performed miracles which Simon had witnessed:

> And the people with one accord gave heed unto those things which Philip spake, hearing and seeing the miracles which he did. For unclean spirits, crying with a loud voice, came out of many that were possessed with them: and many taken with palsies, and that were lame, were healed. And there was

great joy in the city (Acts 8:6-8).

It is likely that Simon did not see those who received the Holy Spirit perform miracles of healing or cast out demons. Simon had already witnessed these "common" things in the ministry of Philip (Acts 8:6-7). Nor did he see simply an expression of "joy in the Holy Spirit," since the miracles through the ministry of Philip had brought great joy: "And there was great joy in the city" (Acts 8:8). Simon likely saw and heard something that he had not seen or heard before. But, what did Simon see and hear? Many Classical Pentecostals conclude that Simon witnessed the same manifestation that occurred on the day of Pentecost. They believe that he saw and heard the Samaritan disciples speaking in tongues.

Did Simon want the power to lay his hands on people and transmit to them the Holy Spirit *with the evidence of speaking in tongues*? If this was not what it was that he *saw and heard*, then why did he not bargain with *Philip* for the power earlier? Why now, all of a sudden, would he be interested in the power that he had seen and heard all along?

It seems obvious that Simon saw something visible and conspicuous. Why else would the Scriptures record these words, "And when Simon saw that through the laying on of the apostles' hands the Holy Ghost was given"? Since Simon saw something he had not seen up to that time and offered to purchase it, it is arguable that what he saw (and heard) was speaking in other tongues. For many Classical Pentecostals, it appears that a preponderance of the evidence leads to this conclusion in the Samaritan/Simon experience.

The Third Occasion: Paul's Spirit Baptism
Acts 9

Many Pentecostals use Paul's baptism as part of the overall argument for tongues as the initial, physical evidence of the baptism in the Holy Spirit. The argument goes something like this:

> Though it is not recorded that Paul spoke in tongues at the time that he was filled with the Spirit (in Acts 9:17-18), we know that he did in fact speak in tongues because he says so in 1 Corinthians 14:18: "I thank God that I speak in tongues more than you all."

So, of the five, this is the most silent on tongues being the outward manifestation of the baptism in the Holy Spirit, but Paul himself later (1 Corinthians 14:18) says that he spoke in tongues.

However, an astounding point arises here. Had Paul not dealt with the *tongues issue* in the Corinthian church, we would not have ever known that he spoke in tongues at all. For it is *only* within this Corinthian context that Paul talks about his own gift of speaking (and singing) in tongues (1 Corinthians 14:13-18). Again, how important to Paul could it possibly have been to "get the word out" about speaking in tongues when he himself mentioned his giftedness in only a corrective missive to the Corinthians?

The Fourth Occasion: The Cornelius Experience
Acts 10

Here is a passage that needs little argument. This passage and related texts give us evidence beyond a reasonable doubt. Cornelius and his household received the baptism in the Holy Spirit as Peter preached to them (Acts 10:44-46). The first outward evidence that they had been baptized in the Holy Spirit was that they spoke in tongues (10:46). But, it can also be argued, and I think with more exegetical ground, that the first physical evidence that they had been *saved* was that they spoke in tongues (10:46). Peter was so convinced that speaking in tongues was the evidence that these Gentiles had received the Holy Spirit (thus, salvation) that he challenged: "Can anyone keep these people from being baptized with water? They have received the Holy Spirit just as we have" (10:47).

The Fifth Occasion: The Ephesian Disciples
Acts 19

Here is another occasion in which those who received the baptism in the Holy Spirit spoke in tongues. "When Paul placed his hands on them, the Holy Spirit came on them, and they spoke in tongues and prophesied" (Acts 19:6).

Deductions and Inferences

In three of these five cases, speaking in tongues is clearly an accompaniment of the baptism in the Holy Spirit (see Acts 2:4; 10:44-46; and 19:6). There is nothing circumstantial here. The baptism in the Holy Spirit was accompanied by speaking in tongues.

In another case, Acts 8:14-17 (the second occasion—the Samaritan Experience), circumstantial evidence leads many to conclude that the Samaritans also spoke in tongues, but this is an assumptive conclusion, and one, I might add, that must be arrived at with no help from Luke.

The last case, Acts 9 (the third occasion—Paul's baptism in the Holy Spirit), is the weakest of all. In this passage Paul does not speak in tongues. Although, he did so later (1 Corinthians 14:18).

The Five Occasions: Briefly in Order of Strength

Acts 2:4	*Tongues Accompaniment*
Acts 10:44-46	*Tongues Accompaniment*
Acts 19:6	*Tongues Accompaniment*
Acts 8:14-17	*Circumstances lead some to conclude that they spoke in tongues*
Acts 9:17	*No mention of tongues—tongues later*

If there were in fact three explicit tongues-speaking incidents out of a total of five, that would be fairly strong (deductive) evidence. However, if there are more instances than these five in which people received the infilling of the Holy Spirit and speaking in tongues is not mentioned, the argument for tongues as a paradigm gets weaker. And, what was once thought to be a deductive argument is actually an inductive argument.

It does no good to chide the Classical Pentecostal with the words, "You've reached a hasty generalization by poor inductive reasoning." One must *prove* that he has done so. If the Pentecostal believes, and he does, that he has a total of only five occasions of Holy Spirit baptism in which three explicitly state that the people spoke in tongues and one is very strongly implied, then he is seeing his argument as a legitimately deductive one.

Only Five?

However, there are more than only five occurrences in the book of Acts in which people received the Holy Spirit. Classical Pentecostals have been conditioned to see the baptism in the Holy Spirit as a subsequent work of grace. For them, it is first conversion by faith, and then the subsequent work (also by grace) of the baptism in the Holy Spirit with the evidence of that baptism being the outward manifestation of speaking in other tongues. In reality, however, the tongues-as-evidence argument commits the logical fallacy of *begging the question*.

Begging the question is not, as is popularly thought, "begging for a follow-up question." It is, rather, an argument where the conclusion is "embedded" in the premise. It ends up being a circular argument because the conclusion becomes the premise. The Classical Pentecostal argument starts with just such an impregnated premise. It goes something like this:

> *The Baptism in the Holy Spirit always leads to speaking in tongues.* So, how do we know that many of the people in the book of Acts did not receive the baptism in the Holy Spirit at the time of their conversion experience? Because, they did not speak in tongues.

Thus, by referring to the lack of tongues as evidence, there is an implied assumption that the evidence of the baptism in the Holy Spirit is speaking in tongues. Yet, this is the very thing that must be proven, not simply asserted as is done in their premise.

So, it is important to see clearly, and biblically, that many people (thousands) throughout the book of Acts are depicted as having received the "promise of the father," i.e., the baptism in the Holy Spirit, and yet Luke does not record that they spoke in tongues. Therefore, even though Luke does not specifically mention the words "baptism in the Holy Spirit," this baptism nonetheless transpires when one becomes a Christian. Perhaps the strongest argument for this is in Acts 2:41: "Those who accepted his message were baptized, and about three thousand were added to their number that day." (Please see Acts 2:41 under Argument # 1: Authorial Intent — What was Luke Trying to Convey?)

In this passage (Acts 2:41) three thousand people came to faith in Jesus Christ. Peter said in his sermon (v. 38-39) that if they would repent and be baptized in the name of Jesus Christ for the forgiveness of their sins, then they too would "receive the gift of the Holy Spirit." We must face a thorny question: Did they "receive the gift of the Holy Spirit" as Peter said they would, or did they not? Logic demands (and Luke's account implies) that they did receive the "gift of the Holy Spirit," i.e., they were baptized in the Holy Spirit, just as the 120 in Acts 2. But, Luke does not mention tongues with regard to their reception of the Holy Spirit.

Furthermore, if they did speak in tongues as the initial, physical evidence of this baptism, why does Luke not record the outward phenomena? Whether they all did speak in tongues or not, the point is this: We have just added another occasion to the "deductive argument," which now makes it three of six. Whether all three thousand spoke in tongues or not is not the issue. The issue is that Luke does *not say* if they spoke in tongues, yet it is implied by the context that they *did* receive the "gift of the Holy Spirit," i.e., they were baptized in the Holy Spirit.

Furthermore, instead of being able to say that there were 120 people who were baptized in the Holy Spirit on the day of Pentecost and all of the 120 spoke in tongues (a deductive argument), it must now be admitted that 3,120 people were baptized in the Holy Spirit on the day of Pentecost, and the Scripture only records that 120 spoke in tongues. Attempting to prove a pattern from a mere 120 out of 3,120 is an inductive argument culminating in a hasty generalization. It cannot be logically nor exegetically argued that all Christians who are baptized in the Holy Spirit should speak in tongues from a small sampling of only 120 out of 3,120 people.

Next, when the entire book of Acts is considered, instead of having three out of five occurrences, there are three out of twenty-six references to people being saved/baptized in the Holy Spirit. For the sake of clarification, these references are listed below in a table. Those passages with explicit references to speaking in tongues are on the right hand side, and those passages which speak of those being saved/baptized in the Holy

Spirit with no mention of tongues are listed on the left hand side of the table.

Three out of Twenty-six In Acts

No mention of tongues	Explicit mention of tongues
2:38-41 number of people, 3,000 2:46-47 number of people, unknown 5:14 number of people, unknown 6:1 number of people, unknown 6:7 number of people, unknown 8:12 number of people, unknown 8:15-23 number of people, unknown 8:36, 38-39 number of people, 1 9:17-20 number of people, 1 9:31 number of people, unknown 9:35 number of people, unknown 11:21 number of people, unknown 13:12 number of people, 1 13:48 number of people, unknown 14:1 number of people, unknown 14:21 number of people, unknown 16:5 number of people, unknown 16:14-15 number of people, unknown 16:29-34 number of people, unknown 17:4 number of people, unknown 17:12 number of people, unknown 17:34 number of people, unknown 18:8 number of people, unknown	2:1-4 number of people, 120 10:44-48 of people, unknown 19:6 number of people, 12

The Percentages

Three out of five is sixty percent. Add to that the one perhaps implied text, and there is a possible eighty percent. Thus, according to the Classical Pentecostal argument, there is a *biblical pattern* of people speaking in tongues as the evidence of the baptism in the Holy Spirit *sixty to eighty percent* of the time. If this were true, then it would indeed be a deductive and fairly strong argument.

However, as discovered by even a quick review of the evidence in the table above, there are not three out of five references but three out of twenty-six. So what was thought of as being eighty percent is actually less than twelve percent.

Arguing that the biblical pattern is that all who are baptized in the Holy Spirit should speak in tongues as the initial, physical evidence of that experience is now seen as a hasty generalization from faulty inductive reasoning.

Therefore, the conclusion that all shall speak in tongues when filled with the Holy Spirit simply does not logically follow.

Chapter 7

Argument # 3: The Age to Come

This argument is presented in Gordon Fee's book, *Gospel and Spirit: Issues in New Testament Hermeneutics*. In short, Fee says that to be saved *is to be filled with the Spirit*. To be filled with the Spirit *is to be in the age to come*. When people are not Christians, they are not filled with the Holy Spirit, thus they are not part of the age to come. In brief, Christians are filled with the Holy Spirit by virtue of being Christians.

The age to come[1] is the delightful description that the Bible uses for that future time when all things shall be under Christ's reign. John sums it up well when he says:

> The seventh angel sounded his trumpet, and there were loud voices in heaven, which said: *"The kingdom of the world has become the kingdom of our Lord and of his Christ, and he will reign for ever and ever"* (emphasis added,

Revelation 11:15).

The Bible makes clear a distinction between this present time—the "present evil age" from which we must be rescued (Galatians 1:4)—and the age to come—the time of Christ's manifest rule over all things (Revelation 11:15).

> Grace and peace to you from God our Father and the Lord Jesus Christ, *who gave himself for our sins to rescue us from the present evil age*, according to the will of our God and Father, to whom be glory for ever and ever. Amen (emphasis added, Galatians 1:3-5).

Non-Christians will not take part in the glorious age to come but are subjects of this present evil age. "The god of this age has blinded the minds of unbelievers, so that they cannot see the light of the gospel of the glory of Christ, who is the image of God" (2 Corinthians 4:4). Thus, they shall not enter into Christ's age to come. However, Christians are citizens of two ages. They are *in* the world (i.e., citizens of this present age), but *not of* the world, for they belong to Christ and to the age to come. When Jesus prayed for Christians, he said: "My prayer is not that you take them out of the world but that you protect them from the evil one [the god of this age, 2 Corinthians 4:4]. They are not of the world, even as I am not of it" (John 17:15-16).

However, the age to come has "invaded" this present evil age by the presence of Jesus Christ and the Holy Spirit. And, while Jesus is no longer in this present world in his incarnational form, the Holy Spirit resides in believers and leads and guides them.

> For the grace of God that brings salvation has appeared to all men. It teaches us to say "No" to ungodliness and worldly passions, and to live self-controlled, upright and godly lives *in this present age*, while *we wait for the blessed hope—the glorious appearing* of our great God and Savior, Jesus Christ, who gave himself for us to redeem us from all wickedness and to purify for himself a people that are his very own, eager to do what is good (emphasis added, Titus 2:11-14).

This present age has been "invaded" by God's "incomparably great power" through his Holy Spirit:

> I pray also that the eyes of your heart may be enlightened in order that you may know the hope to which he has called you, the riches of his glorious inheritance in the saints, and his incomparably great power for us who believe. That power is like the working of his mighty strength, which he exerted in Christ when he raised him from the dead and seated him at his right hand in the heavenly realms, far above all rule and authority, power and dominion, and every title that can be given, *not only in the present age but also in the one to come* (emphasis added, Ephesians 1:18-21).

Christians can live godly in this present evil age only by the power of the Holy Spirit. Humans have no ability to do good deeds that hold any weight with God, unless those good deeds are done in the power of the Holy Spirit.

> Command them to do good, to be rich in good deeds, and to be generous and willing to share. In this way they will lay up treasure for themselves as a firm foundation *for the coming age*, so that they may take hold of the life that is truly life (emphasis added, 1 Timothy 6:18-19).

So, the invasion is on, and God's power is present. People can actually experience God's power today in this present evil age, but they do so only through the presence of the Holy Spirit in their lives.

> It is impossible for those who have once been enlightened, who have tasted the heavenly gift, who have shared in the Holy Spirit, who have tasted the goodness of the word of God and *the powers of the coming age*, if they fall away, to be brought back to repentance, because to their loss they are crucifying the Son of God all over again and subjecting him to public disgrace (emphasis added, Hebrews 6:4-6).

Therefore, a Christian is one who has the Holy Spirit residing in him or her, and *the Holy Spirit has initiated that person into the age to come.* Thus, these Christians are citizens of a time yet to come, the age to come. They have the Holy Spirit living in them, and he gives them the "power of the age to come." For now, however, they live in this present evil age as agents of change and messengers of the gospel of Christ.

Having the Holy Spirit

Classical Pentecostals have never denied that Christians have the Holy Spirit in them and the Holy Spirit has initiated them into the age to come. Where they diverge from this argument is the next step.

What does it mean to have the Holy Spirit? According to the *Age to Come Argument*, it means to be *baptized* in the Holy Spirit. But, to the Classical Pentecostal, it means "having the Holy Spirit live inside" a person by virtue of conversion, but this is not the same as being *baptized* in the Holy Spirit or *filled* with the Holy Spirit. Thus, Classical Pentecostals make a distinction between "having the Holy Spirit" (which all Christians do) and "being filled (or baptized) with (or in) the Holy Spirit" (which is evidenced by speaking in tongues).

Classical Pentecostals do not deny that non-tongues-speaking Christians "have" the Holy Spirit, but they do deny that non-tongues speakers have been *baptized in* the Holy Spirit. They sometimes use this analogy: If one drinks a glass of water, he has water in him; but if he completely submerges himself under water, then he has water all around him, and such is the difference between the Holy Spirit being *in a person* and that person *being baptized in the Holy Spirit*.

Therefore, the question one must ask is this, "What are the *requirements* to be baptized in the Holy Spirit?" To the Classical Pentecostal the *requirements* are (1) be saved, and (2) subsequently seek the baptism in the Holy Spirit, realizing that the baptizer in the Holy Spirit is Jesus Christ Himself (Matthew 3:11). And, of course, the evidence that this has taken place is that the Christian shall speak in tongues. So, for the Classical Pentecostal, the baptism in the Holy Spirit is a work of grace subsequent to one's conversion experience. This subsequent experience may happen immediately after conversion or it might happen years after conversion.

But is this a correct view? What does the Bible establish as the "requirements" to be baptized in the Holy Spirit?

You Shall Receive the Gift of the Holy Spirit

On the Day of Pentecost, when the Holy Spirit was poured out upon the 120 in the upper room, many Jews heard the 120 speaking in tongues, and in Acts 2:12 they asked, "What is this?" Peter answers their question by explaining to them that they were witnessing the outpouring of the Holy Spirit (i.e., the gift of the Holy Spirit), and that this was predicted by the prophet Joel. Then Peter says,

> Repent, and let each of you be baptized in the name of Jesus Christ for the forgiveness of your sins; and you shall receive the gift of the Holy Spirit. For the promise is for you and your children, and for all who are far off, as many as the Lord our God shall call to Himself (Acts 2:38-39).

Thus, the *biblical* requirements to be baptized in the Holy Spirit are simple: accept Jesus Christ as Messiah. So, therefore, when one repents and comes to Christ in faith, the *automatic* result is that the person receives the "gift of the Holy Spirit," the same as the 120 did. What is it that the Holy Spirit does for a person at the point of conversion? He fills the person with his presence, and he initiates the person into the age to come (i.e., Christ's kingdom, Colossians 1:13-14). It is, if you will, a "package deal." One does not receive Christ and not receive the gift of (or baptism in) the Holy Spirit.

The dual idea that there are Christians who are "spirit-filled" and Christians who are not "spirit-filled" is an idea that is foreign to the New Testament. Nowhere in either Acts or the epistles is the idea taught that there are some Christians who do not have the baptism in the Holy Spirit, as is commonly taught today by Classical Pentecostals. If one is a Christian, he has been baptized in the Holy Spirit; in fact, it is this gift of the Holy Spirit that separates him from the world and makes him a Christian. "Don't you know that you yourselves are God's temple and that God's Spirit lives in you" (1 Corinthians 3:16)? Is this passage referring to all Christians, or just those who supposedly have the subsequent baptism in the Holy Spirit? "Now it is God who makes both us and you stand firm in Christ. He anointed us, set His seal of ownership upon us, and put His Spirit in our hearts as a deposit, guaranteeing what is to come" (2 Corinthians 1:21-22). Do all, or only some, Christians have the Holy Spirit in their hearts? "You, however, are controlled not by the sinful nature but by the Spirit, if the Spirit of God lives in you. And if anyone does not have the Spirit of Christ, he does not belong to Christ" (Romans 8:9).

All Christians Have the Holy Spirit

Now, in all fairness, it must be pointed out that Classical Pentecostals do *not* contend that one does not have the Holy Spirit at all if he has not been "baptized in the Holy Spirit" (with the initial, physical evidence of speaking in other tongues). They believe that all Christians "have" the Holy Spirit, just not in "fullness." So, non-Pentecostals should not conclude that Pentecostals promote such an aberrant teaching.[2] Classical Pentecostals teach that the moment one is converted and accepts Jesus Christ as his Savior, the Holy Spirit immediately takes up residence in the person, and that person is "a temple of the Holy Spirit" (1 Corinthians 3:16). However, the Classical Pentecostal argues that this immediate indwelling of the Holy Spirit is not the same thing as the *baptism* in the Holy Spirit.

Classical Pentecostals are forced to use non-biblical terminology and examples to explain the difference between the immediate indwelling of the Holy Spirit at conversion and the so-called subsequent *baptism in* the Holy Spirit. Examples such as the difference in drinking water and being completely submerged under water as mentioned above. One Classical Pentecostal colleague explained that the difference was not one of measure, but one of relationship. Just as a young man has a relationship with his fiancée, that relationship changes and is deeper when she becomes his wife. So, while one explanation depends upon *quantity*, the other depends upon *quality*. Yet, neither of these distinctions (nor explanations) is to be found in the New Testament.

Granted, not everything is clearly explained in the New Testament, and sometimes one must arrive at educated conclusions based upon proper research and inferential exegesis. But, if there is an explanation that fits the text better, it should be given serious consideration, and there is. That explanation is simply, as Peter promised, as Joel promised, and as the Holy Spirit led them both to teach, that those in the last days who come to the Lord in faith shall receive the gift of the Holy Spirit, i.e., the baptism in the Holy Spirit.

To conclude otherwise is to argue that some Christians, though saved, have not received the gift of the Holy Spirit in the same way and fashion as did the 120 in the upper room on the Day of Pentecost *even though that is precisely what Peter said they would receive* if they would only repent and believe. Gordon Fee argues that for these early believers there was no distinction between getting saved and being filled with the Holy Spirit. He points out that these early Christians would have found the Pentecostal phrase "Spirit-filled Christian" an oddity because there are no other types of Christians. If you are a Christian, you are filled with the Spirit. He says that this would be as redundant as saying a "Scandinavian Swede."[3] These early believers simply did not see salvation and Holy Spirit baptism as two separate stages.

A "Scandinavian Swede," a "Spirit-filled Christian"— the redundancy is obvious. The reception of the Holy Spirit (as Peter declared it, i.e., to be baptized in the Holy Spirit) is the main ingredient to being a Christian, and that happens to all people who believe in Christ at the time of their conversion, even if they do not speak in other tongues.

A Paradigm Was Established

Furthermore, since the birth of the church happened with the outpouring of the Spirit on the Day of Pentecost, and since Peter proclaimed (a didactic portion of Scripture) that all who believed would receive the gift of the Holy Spirit, and since all of the three thousand on Pentecost received the Holy Spirit in the same fullness as the 120 had and just as Peter said would happen, then it cannot be denied that *a paradigm was established*. However, it is not the paradigm of baptism in the Holy Spirit with the evidence of speaking in tongues. Rather, the paradigm was (and continues to be) "repent and accept Jesus and *automatically* receive the baptism in the Holy Spirit." Just as Luke did not make a point of saying that the three thousand spoke in tongues, so one should not get misdirected into missing the true paradigm. Luke's intent was soteriological, and his emphasis was simply this: *All who repent and come to Jesus Christ will receive the gift of the Holy Spirit, and they will be saved. And, subsequently, they will be citizens of the age to come.*

That people coming into the kingdom of God were automatically baptized in the Holy Spirit is also evident from the situation in Acts 19:2. Paul asks some disciples in Ephesus, "Did you receive the Holy Spirit when you believed?" Why the concern by Paul? Gordon Fee argues that these Ephesians (at this time) were obviously not Christians because they did not have the Spirit.[4]

The infilling of the Holy Spirit (or baptism or gift of

the Holy Spirit) is promised to all who repent and accept Jesus Christ as Savior. If one is saved, then he has the Spirit of God. The New Testament church saw the baptism in the Holy Spirit as an integral part of what it meant to be "saved." Thus, the question is not, "Do people get baptized in the Holy Spirit at conversion?" They do. The question is why do some people who get baptized in the Holy Spirit speak in tongues?

The New Testament never makes the distinction between (1) getting saved and (2) being filled with the Holy Spirit as though they are two entirely different experiences. Throughout the book of Acts, it is obvious that getting saved included being filled with the Spirit. They go hand-in-hand. If one is saved, he is spirit-filled. Thus no New Testament writer says, "Seek the baptism in the Holy Spirit." What is said is: "Repent and be baptized, every one of you, in the name of Jesus Christ for the forgiveness of your sins. And you will receive the gift of the Holy Spirit" (Acts 2:38). The baptism in the Holy Spirit is simply and automatically the fruit of true repentance and saving belief in Jesus Christ.

End Notes

[1] See, for example, Matthew 12:32; Mark 10:30; and Luke 18:30.

² There are, of course, the Oneness Pentecostals who do in fact teach that unless one is "baptized in the Holy Spirit" with the initial, physical evidence of speaking in other tongues, *one is not saved*. However, it is my opinion—and that of many other theologians and apologists—that the Oneness Pentecostals are neither orthodox nor Christians. Their aberrant teachings separate them from true Christianity. They deny the orthodox doctrine of the Trinity and they have a gospel of "works salvation"; thus they are not Christians in the biblical sense, and they are certainly not Christian Pentecostals.

In an article in *Christianity Today* (April 1, 2002), "Jesus Only Isn't Enough," J. Stephen Lang stated that "the National Association of Evangelicals, Pentecostal World Fellowship, and Pentecostal Fellowship of North America rightly find Oneness Pentecostals too far removed from classical orthodoxy to include in their ranks."

The Oneness Pentecostals' teaching on the issue of speaking in tongues does not represent Classical or Traditional Pentecostals. And, it is unfair and unscholarly to equate the heterodox Oneness Pentecostals and their teachings with orthodox, Trinitarian, Classical Pentecostals and their teachings.

Two good resources on this topic are: *Oneness Pentecostals and the Trinity* by Gregory A. Boyd (Baker Book House, 1992), and *Jesus Only Churches* by E. Calvin Beisner (Zondervan Publishing House, 1998).

³ Gordon D. Fee, *Gospel and Spirit: Issues in New Testament Hermeneutics* (Peabody, MA.: Hendrickson Publishers, Inc., 1991), p. 114.

⁴ Ibid.

Chapter 8

Argument # 4: Subsequence

Classical Pentecostals contend that the baptism in the Holy Spirit with the evidence of speaking in tongues is subsequent to conversion.[1] However, the issue still must be authorial intent. Was Luke attempting to convey the idea of subsequence? Here, briefly, are the three Lukan accounts in which people spoke in tongues.

One: Acts 2:4—*On the Day of Pentecost*

Undoubtedly the 120 disciples were saved; they probably had been baptized in water (either by John or by one of the other disciples of Jesus), and on the day of Pentecost they "were all filled with the Holy Spirit and began to speak with other tongues, as the Spirit gave them utterance" (Acts 2:4).

THE SEQUENCE:
- 1. Belief
- 2. Baptized in water
    It should be pointed out that some of the disciples were baptized in water by John the Baptist before coming to know Jesus Himself (John 1:35-42). So, in their cases, they might have actually been baptized in water first, and then came to faith in Jesus later. Thus, they didn't have explicit faith in Christ until after they were water baptized.
- 3. Baptized in the Holy Spirit
- 4. Spoke in tongues

Two: Acts 10—*The Cornelius Experience*
THE SEQUENCE:
- 1. Speaking in tongues
- 2. Belief is inferred as well as Spirit baptism
- 3. Baptized in water

Three: *Acts 19—The Ephesian Disciples*
THE SEQUENCE:
- 1. Baptized in water
- 2. Baptized in the Holy Spirit
- 3. Spoke in tongues

No Modus Operandi

In these three cases, the principals spoke in tongues, *but the sequence of events was not the same.* If there is to be a rigid sequence of events, a *modus operandi*, then why does Luke not make this clear? At least, why not make it consistent? Another key issue is that out of twenty-eight chapters reporting on literally thousands of conversions of people coming to faith in Jesus Christ, why *only three* explicit references to speaking in tongues? And why are these three not consistent with each other? In the Cornelius case, the Jewish Christians were stunned. In fact, the passage says:

> While Peter was still speaking these words, the Holy Spirit fell upon all those who were listening to the message. And all the circumcised believers who had come with Peter were amazed that the gift of the Holy Spirit had been poured out upon the Gentiles also" (emphasis added, Acts 10:44-45).

In this case, the Gentiles did not express explicit faith in Jesus Christ. They had not been baptized in water first. They had not gone through any Jewish rites of conversion. The Jewish Christians who were there did not see these Gentiles go through the "normal steps of conversion." There was no formal "altar call."

Pentecostals simply place too great an emphasis upon the *modus operandi*. Not only does Luke *not* attempt to establish a pattern of tongues as evidence of the baptism in the Holy Spirit, or as a step within some rigid sequential framework, but in the overwhelming majority of conversion experiences throughout the book of Acts, he does not even mention tongues or their place in the *modus operandi*. In fact, *nowhere does Luke explicitly talk about sequence.*

Fee agrees and says that since there are diversity of patterns within the book of Acts, how are Christians to know which one of them is to be normative? Furthermore, if normativeness had been Luke's concern, he would have clearly made that apparent, but he does not.[2]

"Sequence" is inferred by Classical Pentecostals from the scant references to tongues in relationship to the baptism in the Holy Spirit. Without a doubt, Luke has far less to say about sequence than do many Classical Pentecostals.

End Notes

[1] A clarification should be made at this point. The subsequent blessing of the baptism in the Holy Spirit as taught by Classical Pentecostals is not to be confused with the common second-blessing theology which ascribes a once-for-all, post-conversion, entire sanctification, i.e., the eradication of all sin. In brief, the distinction made is the difference between some Pentecostal-holiness groups (second-blessing theology) and the Classical Pentecostal groups, such as the Assemblies of God (who simply believe in a subsequent blessing of Holy Spirit baptism, but not with the sanctification baggage of the Pentecostal-holiness groups). Classical Pentecostals are closer to their Reformed evangelical brethren on sanctification.

[2] Fee, *Gospel and Spirit*, p. 103.

Chapter 9

Argument # 5: Historical Narrative Versus Didactic

Proper biblical hermeneutics[1] always plays a major part in biblical interpretation. One primary hermeneutical principle that is especially germane to this discussion is historical narrative versus didactic (teaching) portions of Scripture.[2] Since there are different *genres* of literature in Scripture, each must be seen in its own context and interpreted in light of its own literary principles.

To be sure, there is a difference between historical narrative and didactic genres, and it is important to know which is which and to know how to interpret them accordingly. But, an oversimplified view is that doctrines can *only be derived from didactic portions of Scripture* while historical narratives serve *only to show us what transpired for others in those historical events*. Perhaps the best way to clarify this is to give examples of each.

Historical Narrative Example

When the historical narrative in Exodus tells us that Moses struck a rock with his staff and water came out, are we then to assume that all believers can strike a rock to have water? God is speaking to Moses, and he says:

> "I will stand there before you by the rock at Horeb. Strike the rock, and water will come out of it for the people to drink." So Moses did this in the sight of the elders of Israel (Exodus 17:6).

However, one narrative does not a doctrine make. Something must be repeated to establish a norm (a "have-to pattern"). Furthermore, this "thing" must be consistent each time it is repeated. It is interesting that this "water from a rock" did not happen only once. It happened again. In the book of Numbers, it says:

> Then Moses raised his arm and struck the rock twice with his staff. Water gushed out, and the community and their livestock drank (Numbers 20:11).[3]

However, even with two separate accounts of Moses striking a rock to retrieve water, this narrative *description* of what happened should not be treated as though it were a *prescription* for "the way to get water." And, as far as I know, no thoughtful Christian believes that we can simply take a stick and hit a rock for our water needs.

Though this is an extreme example of how not to build doctrines on narratives, the point should be clear.

Narrative passages of Scripture are often only *descriptive*, i.e., describing how some people did something and not *prescriptive*, i.e., prescribing how all people must do something.

Didactic Example

Now, let's review a didactic portion of Scripture.

> If anyone speaks in a tongue, two—or at the most three—should speak, one at a time, and someone must interpret. If there is no interpreter, the speaker should keep quiet in the church and speak to himself and God (1 Corinthians 14:27-28).

In this didactic (teaching) portion of Scripture, Paul is addressing the Corinthians, and he is explaining to them how they should conduct their worship service. Since this is a *direct teaching*, we can see and accept its universal application for all Christians for all times. When something is for all Christians for all times, then we call that a "norm" (or "normative"). It is something that should (must) be done by all Christians, and when they do not do it, they are out of line.

However, in our narrative passage of Moses and the rock, we would not see that as a norm. The water-from-the-rock situation was unique to Moses. Nowhere is there a didactic portion of Scripture that commands all Christians to strike rocks for water. Therefore, it is not a "norm." It is simply a record (narrative) of how God dealt with Moses in particular times at particular places.

Two More Examples

It appears that Peter had a particular ministry that was unique to him. The historical narrative of the book of Acts gives us this account:

> As a result, people brought the sick into the streets and laid them on beds and mats so that at least Peter's shadow might fall on some of them as he passed by (Acts 5:15).

Peter had a "Shadow Ministry,"[4] and no one assumes that this is a norm. This passage is *not prescribing* how Christians are to heal the sick; it is simply recounting this unique experience in Peter's life.

Speaking of Peter, he himself, however, writes didactically to all Christians when he says,

> Therefore, rid yourselves of all malice and all deceit, hypocrisy, envy, and slander of every kind. Like newborn babies, crave pure spiritual milk, so that by it you may grow up in your salvation, now that you have tasted that the Lord is good (1 Pet. 2:1-3).

In this passage Peter gives instructions that are normative for all Christians for all time. Unlike Moses' rock-and-water experience, which is only descriptive, Peter's instructions are prescriptive. Here is a simple table that may help clarify the two.

NARRATIVE	and	**DIDACTIC**
A story		A teaching
Descriptive		Prescriptive
Normal for some		A norm for all

The Twist

However, it is not as simple as saying, "Doctrines can only be derived from didactic portions of Scripture and never narrative portions of Scripture." If the discussion were that simple, we would be able to simply state that the book of Acts is a historical narrative, and, thus, no doctrines can be built from it. That then, would end the debate. But, the church has legitimately established some of its doctrines and practices via historical narrative. As Fee points out, the Baptists (and some others) insist on baptism by immersion. This practice, however, is not based on any clear didactic portion of Scripture, but rather upon a word study of the word *baptize* and upon historical narrative. Why does the church meet each Sunday for services? What didactic portion of Scripture establishes that routine for our church practice? Upon what New Testament didactic portion of Scripture does the church teach and support the practice of tithing?

Furthermore, New Testament writers did use Old Testament narratives for didactic instruction. In fact, Paul seems to imply as much when he says, "All Scripture is God-breathed and is useful for teaching, rebuking, correcting and training in righteousness, so that the man of God may be thoroughly equipped for every good work" (2 Timothy 3:16-17). Also, in Romans 15:4, Paul says, "For everything that was written in the past was written to teach us, so that through endurance and the encouragement of the Scriptures we might have hope." So, historical narrative does have didactic value; the issue is how do we legitimately exegete doctrine and practice from historical narrative?

If we conclude that doctrines *may* be derived from historical narrative (and I do), we cannot then *simply* say, "Well, there you go. Since we can use that hermeneutical principle, then speaking in tongues is the initial, physical evidence of the baptism in the Holy Spirit." You see, even when we conclude that doctrines can be built from historical narratives, shall we then institute the "water-from-rocks ministry," or the "shadow-healing ministry"? Obviously not.

In *Paraclete,* Roger Stronstad gives a weighty argument for "The Biblical Precedent for Historical Precedent"[5] (i.e., building doctrines from narratives). However, in the same issue of *Paraclete,* Gordon Fee supplies a strong rejoinder in which he offers several cautions concerning this hermeneutical principle.[6] In essence, if doctrines are to be built upon narrative portions of Scripture, many caveats come into play. After an ongoing discussion on this topic, Gordon Fee eloquently expresses my concern:

> At issue, as I perceive it, is whether historical precedent may serve in a *normative way* for the establishing of Christian doctrine. I have expressed concern on this issue; and as Roger [Stronstad] has indicated, "considerable criticism" has been levied against my

> articulation of things. But I must confess that in all of that criticism, *I have failed to find a hermeneutical articulation that took me by the hand and showed me how one goes about doing this—that is, establishing something normative on the basis of historical precedent alone* (emphasis added).[7]

So, while there may be legitimacy in building doctrine from narrative passages alone, there is yet to be a definitive hermeneutical statement on how that is properly done.

I believe that it is shortsighted to simply reject a teaching out of hand because it is derived from historical narrative. It is my position that doctrines and practices may be legitimately derived from historical narratives. However, this position notwithstanding, I still must express two caveats: (1) There has been no definitive, accepted method of determining doctrine from narrative alone, and (2) the historical narrative of Acts does not seem to *significantly demonstrate* the idea that speaking in tongues is the norm for the baptism in the Holy Spirit.

So, while I accept the view that historical narrative is grounds for doctrine and practice, it must make that doctrine and practice obvious. And, the reality is—as demonstrated in chapter five—Luke simply does not do that. He does not make tongues as evidence obvious. He gives only three references to speaking in tongues out of twenty-six conversion accounts. Not only are there only three, but each of them is inconsistent with the other. Thus, it seems obvious, at least to this researcher, that this is one doctrine that cannot be adequately exegeted from the narrative.

The fact that Luke gives three accounts in which people spoke in tongues in association with the baptism in the Holy Spirit is not to be discarded, but neither is it to be elevated to a theological dogma. Truth certainly can be gleaned from historical narrative, but one must be careful not to draw universal, conclusive norms based on *occasional happenings* within the historical narratives. Luke's account seems to indicate that speaking in tongues is a normal Christian experience, but the account does not provide an adequate exegetical basis to make it a norm.

A Non Sequitur

That some people spoke in tongues when they were saved and filled with the Holy Spirit is a fact of record. This is a truth to be gleaned from the historical narrative that Luke supplies. That the gift of tongues has *not* ceased is also a fact of record, both biblical and historical. That this is a repeatable phenomenon, i.e., that people today can repeat the biblical experience of speaking in tongues, is also true.

So, while I believe that speaking in tongues is legitimately repeatable, and it is a normal Christian experience, I do not think that the Acts narrative imposes (or teaches) that all Christians must speak in tongues when they are saved and filled with the Holy Spirit. That tongues as evidence of the baptism in the Holy Spirit is a universal "norm" is simply a *non sequitur*. It simply *does not follow* from the historical narrative that Luke supplies.

Had Luke made a point of clearly, repetitiously, and consistently depicting throughout the book of Acts that *all* who were saved and filled with the Holy Spirit spoke in tongues, then there would be a paradigm (norm) that we would have to follow. Even if he had clearly and consistently depicted that *most* of them did, it would make a strong argument for tongues-as-evidence. However, this is not the case. Luke's record indicates that less than twelve percent of the people who were saved throughout the book of Acts spoke in tongues. This is a small percentage indeed.

Since Luke mentions so few who spoke in tongues as evidence of their conversion/infilling with the Holy Spirit, this clearly indicates that speaking in tongues was *not* a major point that he was attempting to develop. Thus, speaking in tongues as evidence of the baptism in the Holy Spirit *as normative* is not a doctrine that can be legitimately derived from the historical narrative known as the book of Acts.

End Notes

[1] Biblical hermeneutics is simply defined as the art and science of biblical interpretation.

[2] I will only briefly touch upon this topic as others (Fee and Stronstad, for examples) have dealt with this topic extensively and the reader is directed to their works

in this area. See Fee, *Gospel and Spirit*, and Roger Stronstad, *The Charismatic Theology of St. Luke*. See also Roger Stronstad, "The Biblical Precedent for Historical Precedent" in *Paraclete*, vol. 27, no. 3, 1993, pp. 1-10; and Gordon D. Fee, "Response to Roger Stronstad's 'The Biblical Precedent for Historical Precedent'" *Paraclete*, vol. 27, no. 3, 1993, pp. 11-14. I lean heavily toward Fee's assessment of this issue and give the gist of that argument in this chapter.

[3] Of course there are theological differences in these two stories which are significant and interesting but not germane to this book. For further study on this, note the consequences visited upon Moses for striking the rock a second time and compare 1 Corinthians 10:4 and Hebrews 6:6.

[4] As I recall, I first heard the phrase "Shadow Ministry" in regard to Peter from A/G pastor Rev. Kerry McRoberts during his lecture, "The Dangers of Spiritual Fog."

[5] Stronstad, "The Biblical Precedent for Historical Precedent," *Paraclete* (Summer 1993): pp. 1-10.

[6] Gordon D. Fee, "Response to Roger Stronstad's 'The Biblical Precedent for Historical Precedent,'" *Paraclete* (Summer 1993): pp. 11-14.

[7] Ibid., 11.

Chapter 10

History: Not on the Side of Evidence

Some have attempted to argue that speaking in tongues ended with the death of the original disciples and apostles. Some argue that speaking in tongues did not continue on throughout the history of the church, and the speaking in tongues that we now see in the church only started at the turn of the 20th century. However, such is simply not the case.

It has been clearly shown by historians and researchers that tongues speaking was not absent from the church throughout the last 2,000 years. Though it did not have the overwhelming presence that it does today, it was never "done away with" throughout the church's history. There have been many documented cases over the years in which Christians spoke in tongues. To deny this is to be selective about church history, which becomes a case of special pleading. However, there is one aspect concerning the tongues issue that *is* absent from church history: the *connection* of the baptism in the Holy Spirit with speaking in tongues.

Tongues As Evidence a Recent Development

It is a little known fact among average Classical Pentecostals that the tongues-as-evidence doctrine is a relatively recent development. Only a couple of times through my years as a Christian have I heard tongues-as-evidence proponents point out that this doctrine is a recent one. And, in these few times it has come from scholars through the printed medium. Whenever I have spoken to my Pentecostal colleagues about this issue, they often speak of the doctrine as if the apostles themselves handed it down to their disciples, and they to their disciples, and so on throughout the history of the church. So, it might be an eye opener for some to realize that the *tongues-as-evidence doctrine* has no such history. I should point out that simply because something is of recent origin does not necessarily mean that it is wrong. However, if something is relatively new and novel, should not we ask why and how the Christian church "missed it" for nearly two thousand years?

One very clear statement on this issue comes from within Pentecostalism through the book, *Initial Evidence: Historical and Biblical Perspectives on the Pentecostal Doctrine of Spirit Baptism*, edited by Gary B. McGee, professor of church history at the Assemblies of God Theological Seminary. This interesting book is a collection of essays by various scholars. In chapter two, "Evidence of the Spirit: The Medieval and Modern Western Churches," historian Stanley Burgess explains that throughout the history of the church there has always been the idea and teaching of the baptism in the Holy Spirit. However, he goes on to say that throughout this same history there was no *connection* between the baptism in the Holy Spirit and speaking in tongues. In fact, he says that,

> the modern Pentecostal identification of glossolalia as the "initial evidence" of such baptism is completely novel until the nineteenth-century Irvingites. Amazingly, in almost two millennia of Christian life and practice, no one . . . associated tongues with the advent of life in the Spirit.[1]

In fact, not even Edward Irving (1792—1834) made a necessary connection between speaking in tongues and the baptism in the Holy Spirit. In fact, Burgess says that those who argue that Irving did make such a connection are themselves coming to this conclusion by the influence of "their own twentieth-century concepts and terminology."[2]

It is indeed *amazing*, as Burgess says, that during the two thousand years of the church's existence no one connected the baptism in the Holy Spirit with the necessity of speaking in tongues. It simply was not a teaching of the disciples, the early church, or the later church until the turn of the 20th century.

Charles Fox Parham, a 29 year-old college drop out,[3] advanced and popularized the tongues-as-evidence notion around 1901. Now, two things need to be settled early on so that I am not misunderstood. First, the age of Parham, though young, does not disqualify him from either teaching or arriving at correct doctrine through his own study and experience. Second, one does not need a college degree to preach God's truths. But it seems apparent that since no significant individuals or groups in the history of the church made the connection between the baptism in the Holy Spirit and the necessity of speaking in tongues, we should at least pause and seriously reconsider this idea and its origin.

Think carefully for a moment. In almost two thousand years of Christian life and practice, the tongues-as-evidence doctrine simply has no representation. It simply was not taught until about 100 years ago.

It is true that doctrines develop over time. For instance, the doctrine of the Trinity was not fully developed until the fourth century of the church's existence. However, it was an ongoing discussion and in development for several centuries. The same can be said for many of the doctrines of the Christian church. Though they do not come neatly wrapped up with a bow directly from the first century disciples, Christian doctrines for the most part have long and illustrious histories within the church. The tongues-as-evidence doctrine simply does not have such a history. This should at least give us reason to seriously reconsider and reevaluate the doctrine in light of the biblical text, which I believe I have done in this book.

Charles Fox Parham and His Teachings

Charles Parham not only taught and popularized the idea that speaking in tongues was the evidence of the baptism in the Holy Spirit, but he also taught other things that were incorrect. First, he developed the mistaken notion that speaking in tongues was a missionary tool that would prepare missionaries to speak to foreign people without having to learn the languages of those people. Parham taught that tongues were xenoglossa (real languages). There have been many reputable accounts (not the least of which is Acts 2) in which people spoke in tongues and someone recognized the language. However, the idea that the gift of speaking in tongues is a *missionary tool* has no biblical support.

Some have vainly argued that the Jews heard the disciples speaking in their own languages in Acts 2 and thus the tongues-speaking was the preaching of the gospel to them. This is simply a *non sequitur*. Nowhere does the Bible say (didactically) that tongues-speaking is to communicate the gospel to foreign peoples. The argument for this position seems to be based upon the one account in Acts 2, which is a narrative (not a didactic portion of Scripture). Not only is this a narrative, but even within this narrative account, it does not lead the thoughtful exegete to conclude that the tongues spoken were the preaching of the gospel. For it was not the disciples' tongues-talking that caused people to repent and get saved on that fateful day. In fact just the opposite is true. The tongues-talking solicited mockery from the crowd. Some said, "These people are drunk" (Acts 2:13)!

Please note carefully that Peter *shifted* from speaking in tongues to preaching the gospel in his common language, and that is when people came to accept Christ as the messiah. It wasn't tongues that convinced these people to repent. It was Peter's preaching that convinced them to repent. F. F. Bruce agrees and says that "there is no suggestion" that Peter preached his sermon in tongues.[4]

Many of Parham's followers and students, however, believed this mistaken notion. But it actually went further than that. Parham also taught that those who were baptized in the Spirit with the evidence of speaking in tongues became *instant* missionaries. And furthermore, Parham told these "instant missionaries" that they were humanity's *last generation*.

Next, he taught that they were now "sealed" as members of the bride of Christ (evidenced by speaking in tongues). And because they were thus sealed as members of the bride of Christ, they would be spared the horrors and destruction of the end time tribulation. (Apparently non-tongues talkers would not be spared.) But, of course, they were not the last generation, and the horrors and destruction of the end time tribulation did not happen in their lifetime.

By 1910 most Pentecostals no longer believed that speaking in tongues was a missionary tool nor that it made people instant missionaries. And, most—if not all—of Parham's original audience have since passed away proving that they were not the last generation.[5]

Conclusion

The final point of this chapter is simply to say that history is not on the side of the tongues-as-evidence argument. It is a recent theological development that enjoys no representation in the overall history of the church.

End Notes

[1] McGee, editor, *Initial Evidence*, p. 37.

[2] Ibid, p. 35-36.

[3] See McGee, editor, *Initial Evidence*, p. 59, and Burgess and McGee, *Dictionary of Pentecostal and Charismatic Movements*, p. 660.

[4] F. F. Bruce, gen. ed., *The New International Commentary on the New Testament* (Grand Rapids, MI.: Eerdmans Publishing Co., 1988) *The Book of Acts* by F. F. Bruce, p. 60.

[5] Various arguments have been advanced as to how many years constitute a "generation." Some have argued that it is as little as 20 years, others argue that the Bible indicates that it is 30 or 40 years. Some have even extended it to as many as 60 years. In any case, Parham's teachings that his was the final generation was simply wrong.

Chapter 11

Why Tongues?

On the Day of Pentecost

Why on the day of Pentecost did the 120 who were baptized in the Holy Spirit speak in tongues? First, it was not, *absolutely not,* to preach to others in their own language. Nowhere does the Bible say (nor even imply) that tongues-speaking is to communicate the gospel to other peoples. It was not their tongues-talking that caused people to get saved. In fact, the tongues-talking solicited the crowd's mockery, not repentance. "Some, however, made fun of them and said, 'They have had too much wine'" (Acts 2:13).

As mentioned in the last chapter, it was not until Peter shifted from speaking in tongues to preaching in the common language that people came to accept Christ as the Messiah. F. F. Bruce says that Peter, while likely under divine inspiration, did not preach his sermon in tongues.[1]

Horton agrees and says that Peter spoke in his own language under inspiration of the Spirit.[2]

Why then did the disciples speak in tongues on the day of Pentecost? Throughout the Old Testament, God placed his Spirit in special people; even this, however, was a rarity. Often, they were prophets or priests. The Israelites knew that God had moved by his Spirit through certain, select individuals. However, God had promised through the prophet Joel that there would come a time when he would no longer limit his Spirit to just a few select individuals. He said that a day would come when he would give his Spirit to all his people.

> And afterward, I will pour out my Spirit on all people. Your sons and daughters will prophesy, your old men will dream dreams, your young men will see visions. Even on my servants, both men and women, I will pour out my Spirit in those days (Joel 2:28-29).

Notice the categories of people Joel includes: sons and daughters (and given the women's role in this society, this was a major change and one that young women no doubt looked forward to); old men and young men; servants (again, this certainly would be a shock to the society at large); both men and women (and again, God indicates that women will be filled with his Spirit—no doubt, the young and old women alike looked back with pride and respect at Deborah—*"Deborah, a prophetess, the wife of Lappidoth, was leading Israel at that time,"* Judges 4:4). Now, they too would have the Spirit of God as the Father had promised.

Thus, the Jews would have both known about and longed for that day, the day when the common person (women and servants also) would be filled with and led by the Spirit of God. These words by Peter struck a deep-seated hope in the hearts of these Jews. But how would they receive this wonderful infilling of the Spirit of the living God? Peter explained to them that it was Jesus Christ who had given this promised gift of the Holy Spirit.

> God has raised this Jesus to life, and we are all witnesses of the fact. Exalted to the right hand of God, he has received from the Father the promised Holy Spirit and has poured out what you now see and hear (Acts 2:32-33).

F. F. Bruce says that the speaking in tongues arrested the attention of the Jews that day, and they were thus ready to listen to the sermon by Peter.[3] While Bruce's idea is obviously true, Stanley Horton adds an insightful perspective on "why tongues" in Acts 2. He says that the various tongues emphasized God's promise to pour out His Spirit upon all flesh.[4] The fact that these Jews from various places heard the 120 disciples speaking in their own languages would indicate to them that God was willing to pour out his Spirit upon them, all of them. Thus, as Horton has well said, the speaking in tongues *highlighted* God's purpose to pour out His Spirit on *all* flesh. A review of this text seems to reinforce Horton's idea. For in this passage, Luke is careful to name the various locations from where these Jews had come.

Acts 2:4-12

> All of them were filled with the Holy Spirit and began to speak in other tongues as the Spirit enabled them. Now there were staying in Jerusalem God-fearing Jews from every nation under heaven. When they heard this sound, a crowd came together in bewilderment, because each one heard them speaking in his own language. Utterly amazed, they asked: "Are not all these men who are speaking Galileans? Then how is it that each of us hears them in his own native language? Parthians, Medes and Elamites; residents of Mesopotamia, Judea and Cappadocia, Pontus and Asia, Phrygia and Pamphylia, Egypt and the parts of Libya near Cyrene; visitors from Rome (both Jews and converts to Judaism); Cretans and Arabs—we hear them declaring the wonders of God in our own tongues!" Amazed and perplexed, they asked one another, "What does this mean?"

What speaking in tongues meant was that God was pouring out his Spirit upon *all mankind*.

Accompaniments of the Baptism in the Holy Spirit

Note also that when Joel spoke of the day when people would be baptized in the Holy Spirit, he said that certain things would accompany this baptism: (1) prophecy, (2) spiritual dreams, and (3) visions. Thus, to the prophet Joel, the outward manifestations of the baptism in the Holy Spirit were not limited to speaking in tongues. And, as has been shown, Peter himself spoke under a divine inspiration (due to the baptism in the Holy Spirit) in the *common language* as he addressed the Jews.

There does not seem to be any indication in Acts 2 that Luke is attempting to establish speaking in tongues as *the* primary, physical evidence of the reception of the promise of the Father (the Holy Spirit). Rather, it appears that tongues served to *catch the attention of the Jews* and to indicate that God *was now pouring his Spirit upon all flesh.*

Even Upon Gentile Flesh

Furthermore, it is reasonable to infer from what happened later in the book of Acts that another purpose of the tongues-talking was so that the Jewish Christians would later be able to recognize in an outward manifestation *God's acceptance of the Gentiles.*

Why doesn't Luke say that all or even some of the other three thousand who were saved on the day of Pentecost spoke in tongues? After all, it is clear that they too "received the gift of the Holy Spirit" (Acts 2:38-39). The primary reason seems obvious: These three thousand were Jews and there was no need to show an outward manifestation of God's acceptance of these people.

Two other reasons seem obvious as well: There was no further need to catch the attention of the onlookers, for the onlookers were now the converts. And, there was no further need for God to signify that he was pouring his Spirit upon all flesh because he was now in the process of doing so.

This does not mean that speaking in tongues

ceased. It means only that there is no necessity for Luke to continue to mention it in this context.

But in Acts the tenth chapter, Luke does mention that the *Gentiles* spoke in tongues. It seems that the main reason they spoke in tongues was so the Jews could see God's acceptance of these former outcasts. Peter said, "Can anyone keep these people from being baptized with water? They have received the Holy Spirit just as we have" (10:47). Clearly, Peter sees the experience of these Gentiles and likens it to the experience that the 120 had on the day of Pentecost. Thus, speaking in tongues was "evidential." It was so that the Jews could see by some outward, physical evidence that God had accepted the Gentiles. God was now pouring his Spirit upon all . . . *all* flesh.

So, far from being a paradigm for all to have to follow, it appears that Luke's mentioning of tongues-speaking had several purposes, each being situational and appropriate for specific occasions. The gift of speaking in tongues is still happening today, and again it is still situational and occasional as God deems fit.

End Notes

[1] F. F. Bruce, p. 60.

[2] Stanley M. Horton, *The Book of Acts* (Springfield,

MO.: Gospel Publishing House, 1981), p. 37.

[3] Bruce, *The Book of Acts,* p. 60.

[4] Horton, *The Book of Acts*, p. 37.

Chapter 12

Are Tongues the Least?

Value by Placement

I am always amused when non-Pentecostals say, "Paul said that tongues was the least of the gifts." Implied therein are two basic concepts: (1) That Pentecostals too often make too much out of the tongues issue, and (2) That since it is the "least of the gifts," we can pretty much ignore it altogether. While the first implication is, sadly, too often true, the second one is false. Not only that, but I'm still looking for the passage in which Paul states, "Tongues is the least of the gifts."

Some have argued that it is implied in Paul's listing of the gifts. "After all, it is listed last," so they argue. Actually, it's not always listed last. Even if it were consistently listed last, an overemphasis upon a sheer itemization would undoubtedly be gratuitous. A review of the lists of gifts below will show that Paul did not necessarily place the gifts in a discernible pattern.

Ephesians 4:11	I Cor. 12:28	I Cor. 12:29-30
Apostles	Apostles	Apostles
Prophets	Prophets	Prophets
Evangelists	Teachers	Teachers
Pastors	Miracles	Miracles
Teachers	Gifts of Healing	Gifts of Healing
	Helps	Tongues
	Governments	Interpretation
	Tongues	

1 Cor. 12:8-10	Romans 12:6-8
Word of Wisdom	Prophecy
Word of Knowledge	Service
Faith	Teacher
Gifts of Healing	Exhorter
Working of Miracles	Giver
Prophecy	Administrator
Discerning of Spirits	Mercy
Tongues	
Interpretation	

Interestingly, in 1 Corinthians 12:8-10 and 1 Corinthians 12:29-30, it is the gift of interpretation that is listed last. If the sheer placement of the gifts in the list indicates their value, then we would have to conclude that there is no need for interpretation since it is even lower than tongues! But, Paul indicates that it is of immense value. In fact, he says,

> If anyone speaks in a tongue, two—or at the most three—should speak, one at a time, and someone must interpret. If there is no interpreter, the speaker should keep quiet in the church and speak to himself and God

(1 Corinthians 14:27-28).

So, under the right set of circumstances, the gift listed last (interpretation) becomes very valuable indeed. Obviously, the gift of interpretation is so important that its presence actually regulates the operation of the gift of tongues in the gathered assembly.

Next, shall we simply conclude that mercy is least since it is listed last in Romans 12? I think that the prophet Micah might be able to help answer that: "He has showed you, O man, what is good. And what does the LORD require of you? To act justly and *to love mercy* and to walk humbly with your God" (emphasis added, Micah 6:8).

Are we to deduce from sheer placement that the gift of teacher is the least of the gifts in Ephesians 4:11? And, note also that it is listed third in some other lists.

Then, we can look at other lists besides gifts. The fruit of the Spirit in Galatians 5:22-23 lists the fruit this way: "But the fruit of the Spirit is love, joy, peace, patience, kindness, goodness, faithfulness, gentleness and self-control." Shall we simply presume that "self-control" is the least of the fruit of the Spirit based solely on the fact that it is listed last?

What of this short list: "And now these three remain: faith, hope and love. But the greatest of these is love" (1 Corinthians 13:13). Which is the greatest in this list? Paul tells us, so we don't have to guess. The greatest of these is the one listed last. It is instructive that the person who made this list, and listed the greatest of the three last, is the same person who listed tongues last or nearly last in some other lists.

What possible hermeneutical principle supports a position of "tongues as least" based upon its position in gifts lists? There is none. Are we to believe that Paul wanted to make such a distinction in his lists? That in some of his lists, the best is last, and in others the worst is last? If so, where does Paul indicate this so we can be sure?

The fact is that the simple order of a list of items (biblically speaking) cannot legitimately be taken as a guide to the rank or importance of the items listed. Note that Paul treats prophecy in 1 Corinthians 14 with high regard, yet he lists it sixth on the list in 1 Corinthians 12:8-10; but hold on, it appears in the number one position in Romans 12:6-8.

Since it is obvious that importance cannot be determined simply by order, what might be the reason that the gift of tongues is consistently listed toward the bottom (not last) of the lists? Gordon Fee suggests that perhaps its position is governed by the fact that it was the primary problem area in the Corinthian church, and *not* because it is inherently the lowest in rank. Perhaps Paul lists the other gifts before tongues to make a point of diversity and balance in ministry.[1]

Slow Down and Smell the Context

We've all been instructed to, "Slow down and smell the roses." This means that we are to take the time to enjoy and appreciate those good things around us. When "doing theology," we must, "Slow down and smell the context." In other words, we need to take the time to enjoy and appreciate the context around our topic of study. For example, some people have argued that Paul says that prophecy is a better gift than tongues. Actually, *in context*, what he says is "in the church I would rather speak five intelligible words to instruct others than ten thousand words in a tongue" (1 Corinthians 14:19). Note the two points here: (1) "In the church," and (2) intelligibility. Paul is talking about speaking in tongues "in the church" or in the gathered assembly. To jump from that context to generalized tongues speaking (prayer language) is simply unwarranted.

In the verse just before, he makes this remarkable claim: "I thank God that *I speak in tongues more than all of you*" (emphasis added, 1 Corinthians 14:18). And, given who he was talking to, this is all the more astounding! If Paul spends that much time speaking in tongues in his private devotions, then how is it that some claim that Paul was implying elsewhere that this gift is of little or no value?

The Value of Tongues

Another puzzling statement that I have both heard and read is that speaking in tongues does not edify the body; therefore, it is of no value. Actually, this is what Paul really said: "He who speaks in a tongue edifies himself, but he who prophesies edifies the church" (1 Corinthians 14:4). One must certainly see Paul's positive emphasis upon prophecy, but one must not gloss over the words, "He who speaks in a tongue edifies himself." This was not a condemnation. This is a positive statement.

When one prays in tongues in his private devotions,

it is personally edifying, just as it is edifying when one prays in his private devotions in his native language. I have actually heard people say that Paul was saying that it is wrong to edify oneself through praying in tongues. But, in the context of this same chapter, Paul says, "I *thank God* that *I speak in tongues* more than all of you" (emphasis added, 1 Corinthians 14:18). Not only does Paul say in verse 4 that one who prays in tongues edifies himself, he also says that he actually *thanks God* that he speaks in tongues! Since we know that Paul would rather speak five intelligible words in the gathered congregation rather than "ten thousand words in a tongue," is it not fair to conclude that Paul's reference to his speaking in tongues is in his private devotions? If not, then Paul was thanking God that he spoke in tongues *in the church* more than all of the Corinthians did! This would be at odds with his statement that he'd rather speak five intelligible words in the church. Also, since it was Paul who set the limit of two or at the most three messages in tongues in the church, we run into a problem. How was Paul able to do all of this tongues speaking in the gathered assembly given the limit that he imposed upon tongues? It seems obvious that Paul's reference to his speaking in tongues is predominantly with regard to his private devotions.

  Not only that, but Paul says that he actually *thanks God* that he speaks in tongues. Thus, he "edifies himself," and he thanks God that he does. If there is an inherent negative in edifying oneself, then why do we have private devotions at all? Why should we read the Bible alone? Do not our private times of prayer and Bible reading edify us when we are alone? When I read the Bible by myself, I edify myself. But, when I read the Bible to the gathered congregation, I edify the church. Should I thus conclude that it is bad, or a negative thing, for me to read the Bible when I am alone?

Also, why would Paul condemn in others what he thanks God for in his private life? If Paul is actually saying that the "edifying of oneself" through speaking in tongues is a bad thing, then his double standard is glaring. The consistent and logical conclusion is simple: To edify oneself in tongues is a good thing.

Paul is not contrasting tongues and prophecy in this passage as "bad and good." Nor is he even contrasting them as "one good and one better." He is simply giving a brief charge of order in the church. Perhaps an earlier statement from Paul will help make my point. In 1 Corinthians 12:15-16, Paul says:

> If the foot should say, "Because I am not a hand, I do not belong to the body," it would not for that reason cease to be part of the body. And if the ear should say, "Because I am not an eye, I do not belong to the body," it would not for that reason cease to be part of the body.

Now, would anyone argue that Paul is saying that the ear is bad and the eye is good? Of course not. When you need to see something, the eye is the "gift" to exercise. But, when you need to hear something, the ears are greater than the eyes. And, in our passage (1 Corinthians 14:4), Paul is not saying that prophecy is good and tongues are bad. He is saying, rather, that one gift edifies only the speaker—which is a good thing—while the other edifies the entire congregation—which is also a good thing. Thus, when alone, one may speak in tongues in his personal devotions, but when in the gathered assembly, it is better to prophesy so that the congregation will be edified. Paul is simply pointing out what these gifts do, and since prophecy is better *in the gathered assembly*, then the Corinthians should seek to prophesy rather than speak in tongues when they are together in worship.

Tongues Plus Interpretation Equal Prophecy
Paul says:

> I would like every one of you to speak in tongues, but I would rather have you prophesy. He who prophesies is greater than one who speaks in tongues, *unless he interprets*, so that the church may be edified (emphasis added, 1 Corinthians 14:5).

Note well the first part of this passage: *"I would like every one of you to speak in tongues."* Does he say that he would rather have them prophesy? Yes. But do not gloss over the first part. So, Paul would like every one of these people to speak in tongues! Even more, however, he would like them to prophesy.

Which is greater, the one who prophesies in the church, or the one who speaks in tongues in the church? Paul clearly says that the one who prophesies is greater, but this is *within the context of the gathered church*. Why is prophecy greater than tongues? Intelligibility. Speaking "ten thousand words in a tongue" in a church service is of no value to the congregation, but "five intelligible words to instruct others" is far better for their benefit (1 Corinthians 14:19). This is exactly why Paul says:

> So it is with you. Since you are eager to have spiritual gifts, try to excel in gifts that build up the church. For this reason anyone who speaks in a tongue should pray that he may interpret what he says (1 Corinthians 14:12-13).

Paul says that we are to "try to excel in gifts that build up the church." Which gifts accomplish that? Those that are intelligible to the body. And, one way to do that for the tongues speaker is to "pray that he may interpret what he says." Some argue that the person giving the message in tongues should not be the one who does the interpreting. Paul does not agree with that idea.[2]

Just when we think that the issue is settled, and we think that he is saying simply that prophecy is better than tongues, Paul tosses the word *unless* into the mix and upsets our flow of thought. "Prophecy is greater than tongues *unless* one interprets the message in tongues so that all may benefit." Why does Paul make this clarification? It's simple. The issue is not prophecy versus tongues; the issue is intelligibility.

Prophecy is not inherently greater than tongues, but it has a function that tongues do not: the edification of the body during community worship. However, tongues *coupled with* interpretation is also intelligible; therefore, the twin gifts of tongues and interpretation have the same value as does prophecy, and that is the edification of the believers because they can understand what's being said.

Are Eyes the Least?

Which of the bodily members is the least? Shall we assume that the eyes are the least because they cannot smell or hear? Shall we assume that the nose is the least because it cannot see or taste? This line of thinking is certainly off target. The best member is the one that is needed at that moment to accomplish the job at hand. Value is determined by practical function, and it varies with the need.

If an ambulance siren is blasting behind me as I am driving down the street, then at that moment my ears are greater than my nose. If the milk I am about to drink has spoiled, my nose is greater than my ears.

This is the same with the gifts. Some gifts are not inherently greater than others. The best gifts are those that are needed at the moment. If I am sick, the *gifts of healing* is greater at that moment for me than the gift of *prophecy*. If I am counseling someone who has deep problem issues, hearing a *word of wisdom* from the Lord is greater at that moment than the gift of tongues. In private prayer time and devotions, tongues is greater than prophecy. *In the church*, with the gathered congregation, prophecy is greater than tongues.

End Notes

[1] Gordon D. Fee. *God's Empowering Presence: The Holy Spirit in the Letters of Paul* (Peabody, MA.: Hendrickson Publishers, Inc., 1994), p. 149.

[2] I do realize the protective nature of not allowing unknown or untested people to give messages in tongues and then interpret them themselves. But the answer to this problem is not having a blanket statement saying that the person giving the message cannot be the interpreter. This goes against the obvious statement of Scripture that the tongues talker should pray for the ability to interpret so that the body can be built up (1 Cor. 14:13). The answer, rather, is to allow only those who are known to the leadership to give messages in tongues at all. And, since these people are already accepted by the leadership, they can then trust the person(s) to interpret the messages appropriately. Typically, the person giving the message does not do the interpreting, but it does happen occasionally, and the practice is supported by Scripture.

Chapter 13

Evidence or Accompaniment?

The term "evidence" with regard to tongues and the baptism in the Holy Spirit is misleading in itself. Why? Because, in the book of Acts the evidential nature of tongues was limited and occasional. Let's review the actual passages in which people spoke in tongues at the time of their conversion/Holy Spirit baptism. And, note well that there are only three such passages.

The First Occasion: The Day of Pentecost
Acts 2:1-4

> When the day of Pentecost came, they were all together in one place. Suddenly a sound like the blowing of a violent wind came from heaven and filled the whole house where they were sitting. They saw what seemed to be tongues of fire that separated and came to

rest on each of them. All of them were filled with the Holy Spirit and began to speak in other tongues as the Spirit enabled them.

Notice the three accompaniments: (1) the sound of wind, (2) tongues of fire, and (3) speaking in tongues. Was just the speaking in tongues the "evidence" that God had filled them with his Holy Spirit? For the sake of argument, let's say yes. What was tongues the evidence of? As was mentioned earlier, Horton has well said that the speaking in tongues *highlighted* God's promise to pour out His Spirit on *all* flesh.[1] So, was speaking in tongues "evidential" in Acts 2? Yes. Evidence of what? It was evidence that God was pouring out his Spirit upon all flesh. However, we must understand that "all flesh" for the Jews meant "all Jewish flesh." Peter tells the people that the prophet Joel had said:

> In the last days, God says, I will pour out my Spirit on all people. Your sons and daughters will prophesy, your young men will see visions, your old men will dream dreams. Even on my servants, both men and women, I will pour out my Spirit in those days, and they will prophesy (Acts 2:17-18).

To the Jews, the "all flesh" is qualified as "all Jewish flesh." Note, "*Your* sons and daughters will prophesy, *your* young men will see visions, *your* old men will dream dreams." This outpouring will be upon "all," even "servants, both men and women." The "all" is certainly understood by the Jews to be all of the Jews (men, women, young, old, and servants).

Then, within this context (just a few verses following), we read this remarkable soteriological statement: "And everyone who calls on the name of the Lord will be saved" (Acts 2:21). Closely associated with the outpouring of the Holy Spirit is salvation.

What the Jews are not yet understanding is that when God says "all flesh" and "everyone who calls on the name of the Lord," he means even those outside the Jewish parameters.

So, why would the Jews need to see "evidential tongues" again? Certainly they no longer need to see "tongues as evidence" that God is pouring out his Spirit upon all Jewish flesh, since he has already established that he has done so.

The Second Occasion: The Cornelius Experience
Acts 10:44-47

> While Peter was still speaking these words, the Holy Spirit came on all who heard the message. The circumcised believers who had come with Peter were astonished that the gift of the Holy Spirit had been poured out even on the Gentiles. For they heard them speaking in tongues and praising God. Then Peter said, "Can anyone keep these people from being baptized with water? They have received the Holy Spirit just as we have."

Was speaking in tongues "evidential" in this passage? Yes.

Evidence of what? It was evidence to the "circumcised believers" that "the gift of the Holy Spirit had been poured out *even* on the Gentiles." Note well their astonishment. They were astonished that the Gentiles had received the Holy Spirit because that meant that God had "granted even the Gentiles repentance unto life" (Acts 11:8). The evidential nature of speaking in tongues on this occasion was *soteriological*. As in Acts 2, God was "evidencing" that he was pouring out his Spirit upon "all flesh," not just "all Jewish flesh." Thus, so far, tongues speaking served as evidence that God was pouring out his Spirit upon all people, Jews and Gentiles alike.

The Third Occasion: The Ephesian Disciples
Acts 19:1-7

> While Apollos was at Corinth, Paul took the road through the interior and arrived at Ephesus. There he found some disciples and asked them, "Did you receive the Holy Spirit when you believed?" They answered, "No, we have not even heard that there is a Holy Spirit." So Paul asked, "Then what baptism did you receive?" "John's baptism," they replied. Paul said, "John's baptism was a baptism of repentance. He told the people to believe in the one coming after him, that is, in Jesus." On hearing this, they were baptized into the name of the Lord Jesus. When Paul placed his hands on them, the Holy Spirit came on them, and they spoke in tongues and prophesied. There were about twelve men in all.

In this passage, those who received the baptism in the Holy Spirit spoke in tongues. But they also prophesied. The question, however, is this: Was the speaking in tongues in this passage "evidential"? The need for evidence of God pouring out his Spirit upon all flesh had been accomplished through the Acts 2 and Acts 10 accounts. Between these two sets of passages, the "all flesh" (Jews and Gentiles) has been established. So, what was the Ephesian disciples' tongues-talking evidence of?

Could it have been evidence that these disciples had simply received the Holy Spirit? After all, Paul had asked them, "Did you receive the Holy Spirit when you believed?" But the passage reveals more. They had received only "John's baptism," and Paul had to explain to them that "John's baptism" was prospective. It looked forward to the fullness in Christ. John's baptism was not the fullness. So, Paul actually introduced them to Jesus, and they were baptized in water. Then, "When Paul placed his hands on them, the Holy Spirit came on them, and they spoke in tongues and prophesied."

Tongues as evidence? Yes, indeed. Of what? Salvation in Jesus Christ. But, let us not stop there. They also prophesied. More evidence? Yes, of course. When these disciples were saved and filled with the Holy Spirit (which is the automatic result of being saved), they showed forth two outward manifestations of the Spirit: they spoke in tongues and prophesied. The evidence was not just tongues and prophecy, and it was not just that they had received the baptism in the Holy Spirit, but, indeed, that they had gotten saved.

Conclusions

So, while I do believe that speaking in tongues is evidential in nature, I do not believe that it is simply evidence of a subsequent work of grace indicating that a person who is already a believer has at that moment been "baptized in the Holy Spirit."

While there are various arguments advanced that "five passages" of Scripture indicate that people spoke in tongues when they were filled with the Holy Spirit, it must be admitted that there are only three passages of Scripture in the book of Acts that explicitly mention speaking in tongues.

In Acts 2 "evidential tongues" seem to be testimony that God is fulfilling Joel's prophecy that he is pouring out his spirit upon all of the Jewish people who repent and come to Christ as Savior.

In Acts 10 "evidential tongues" seem to be attestation that God is saving Gentiles who repent.

In Acts 19 "evidential tongues" do not stand alone. "Evidential prophecy" is equal authentication that these disciples (who had only known of John's baptism) were now in the fullness of Christ, i.e., they were saved.

Anachronistic Polemics

We miss the historical and biblical context when we back jump from our present-day post-salvific, subsequent-infilling with tongues-as-evidence argument to these early disciples' experiences set solidly in a soteriological context. Nowhere throughout Acts (or in any other New Testament book) is the "baptism in the Holy Spirit" spoken of and promoted in the fashion as is done by Classical Pentecostals. The Classical Pentecostals' modern-day polemics for this subsequent, post-salvific, fuller infilling of the Holy Spirit is simply nowhere to be found in the New Testament itself. The Classical Pentecostal argument has arisen and developed over the last 100 (or so) years. In fact, according to the *Dictionary of Pentecostal and Charismatic Movements*, Charles Fox Parham first formulated the tongues-as-evidence idea sometime shortly after 1901. Thus, rather than this idea being a New Testament teaching, or even a historical Christian doctrine, it is a recent development.[2]

Evidence Today

So what of today? If speaking in tongues in the New Testament was evidential of salvation, what is it evidential of today? Rather than "evidence" of either salvation or of the baptism in the Holy Spirit, I believe it is far more accurate to simply see speaking in tongues as an occasional accompaniment of the infilling of the Holy Spirit, which is manifested more often by those who seek that accompaniment.

We must understand that tongues is not a *necessary* accompaniment of the infilling of the Holy Spirit (at the time of salvation). A change of heart, a radical newfound love for God and his word, the fruit of the Spirit, love for the brethren, and many other things can be the evidential accompaniment of one's salvation.

We know that we have passed from death to

life, because we love our brothers. Anyone who does not love remains in death. Anyone who hates his brother is a murderer, and you know that no murderer has eternal life in him. This is how we know what love is: Jesus Christ laid down his life for us. And we ought to lay down our lives for our brothers (1 John 3:14-16).

End Notes

[1] Horton, *The Book of Acts*, p. 37.

[2] Stanley M. Burgess and Gary McGee, *Dictionary of Pentecostal and Charismatic Movements*, Grand Rapids, MI.: Zondervan Publishing House, 1988. See various entries including: "Classical Pentecostalism" and "Parham, Charles Fox."

Chapter 14

A Recapitulation and Concluding Remarks

When the five arguments are seen together as a unified whole, they are highly convincing that speaking in tongues is not the initial, physical evidence of the baptism in the Holy Spirit. It appears, logically so, that the preponderance of the evidence rests with the teaching that speaking in tongues is not the initial, physical evidence of the baptism in the Holy Spirit. A brief restatement of each argument is given below.

Argument # 1
Authorial Intent
What Was Luke Trying to Convey?

Authorial intent covers the entire book of Acts. It is quite obvious that Luke's overall intent was soteriological and not glossolalical. Thus, since Luke gave relatively little importance to the issue of tongues as an evidence,

Christians should follow his lead and not over emphasize something that he did not major on.

Argument # 2
Three Times out of Five?
Does This Establish a Paradigm?

There are more than only five references in the book of Acts from which Christians are to take their cue as to the infilling of the Holy Spirit. Instead of three out of five occurrences (i.e., 60%), there are three out of twenty-six occurrences (i.e., 11.5%). Therefore, arguing that *the biblical norm is that all who are baptized in the Holy Spirit shall speak in tongues as the initial, physical evidence of that experience* is actually a hasty generalization based upon faulty inductive reasoning. The conclusion that all shall speak in tongues does not follow with necessity.

Argument # 3
Age to Come Argument

To be saved *is to be filled with the Spirit*. To be a Christian means to have the Holy Spirit and to be initiated into the age to come. Thus, all Christians are filled with the Spirit, but not all Christians speak in tongues.

Argument # 4
Subsequence

Consider Acts 2:4—the Day of Pentecost, Acts 10—the Cornelius Experience, and Acts 19—the Ephesian Disciples. In these three cases, the principals spoke in tongues, *but the sequence of events was not the same.* If there is to be a normative sequence of events derived from these passages, Luke would have made this consistent and abundantly clear.

Argument # 5
Historical Narrative Versus Didactic

There is a difference between historical narrative and didactic genres. In general, Christians should not build their doctrines upon occasional occurrences within narrative portions of Scripture, but they should build them upon didactic portions of Scripture. The book of Acts is predominantly historical narrative, and all the accounts of people speaking in tongues are historical narrative. These speaking-in-tongues narratives *describe* for us what happened with certain people at certain times, but they do not *prescribe* to us what should happen for all Christians at all times.

History: Not on the Side of Evidence

History is not on the side of the tongues-as-evidence argument. It is a recent theological development that enjoys no representation in the overall history of the church.

Extremes and Balance

It is remarkable how often truth lies somewhere in the middle. Not all extremes are wrong or bad, but many times they are one or the other, or both. There seem to be two extremes with regard to the tongues issue, and both are wrong. One extreme says that speaking in tongues is not for today, and in the book of Acts, speaking in tongues was not an evidence of anything. To this Peter might very well reply: "Can anyone keep these people from being baptized with water? They have received the Holy Spirit just as we have" (Acts 10:47). Clearly, *in this specific case* (and *only in this specific case*) Peter believed that speaking in tongues was the initial, physical *evidence* of the salvation of these Gentiles.

The other extreme says that tongues were and are always the initial, physical evidence of the baptism in the Holy Spirit, and if a Christian does not speak in tongues, he has not been baptized in the Holy Spirit.

Concerning the first extreme, one must do Scripture twisting that would make a cultist blush to arrive at such a conclusion. Of the second extreme, one must "exegete his experience" and "beg the question" to arrive at that conclusion.

However, many who do not speak in tongues have also "exegeted" their experience. Some have said, though with more sophistication, "I once prayed and asked God to give me the gift of tongues, but he didn't. Also, no one in my church speaks in tongues. Therefore, *obviously*, tongues are not for today." Often, the charge that Pentecostals have an experiential theology may be turned back upon the accuser.

Evidence

As stated earlier, the term "evidence" with regard to tongues and the baptism in the Holy Spirit is misleading in itself. In the book of Acts, the evidential nature of tongues was limited and occasional. The use of this term in today's Classical Pentecostal circles is beyond and foreign to the New Testament's concept of "evidential tongues."

Without a doubt, speaking in tongues is the *occasional* physical accompaniment of the baptism in the Holy Spirit (which takes place at the time of initial salvation) in the book of Acts. The book of Acts does not give the exact number of people who spoke in tongues as a result of coming to faith in Jesus Christ. Luke simply does not give that information. That *he does not give that information* is precisely what should caution Christians from reading into the "tongues issue" more than what Luke himself intended.

Ask and Ye Shall Receive

People who seek the manifestations of the Spirit, be they tongues, or prophecy, or words of wisdom, et al., will likely receive from the Lord much of what they seek. Some who anticipate the manifestation of tongues at the reception of salvation and the infilling with the Holy Spirit will often experience speaking in tongues. Those who are not seeking such manifestations will most likely not receive. Since this is the case—one need only take a general survey of Pentecostals and non-Pentecostals to discover this—it must be admitted that personal seeking plays a part in the outward manifestations of the Spirit's presence.

In the average Pentecostal church, anywhere from eighty percent to one hundred percent of the people might speak in tongues. In the average non-Pentecostal church, anywhere from eighty percent to one hundred percent of the people might not speak in tongues. This is true because our personal seeking will play a part in the reception of the various gifts. In Matthew 7:7-11, Jesus says that our Father in heaven will "give what is good *to those who ask Him!*" Note the two "actors" here: *one gives* in response to *one asking*.

Many non-Pentecostals have not spoken in tongues because they have not earnestly asked God for this gift (1 Corinthians 14:1). If one's theology says that speaking in tongues is not for today, then why spend time asking for something that no longer exists? Thus, their theology, in many cases, stops them from "seeking what is good," and *their* experience, or lack thereof, is seen as a confirmation of their preconceived theology. Thus, they have a theology based upon their experience.

The Apostle Paul and Present-Day Preachers

There is a widespread teaching that says that Christians are not to seek the gifts. This is usually accompanied by the catchy phrase, "Don't seek the gift, seek the giver." This sets up a false dichotomy, however. It is not an "either/or": Either you can have the gifts of God, *or* you can have God. This is absurd.

Paul says in 1 Corinthians 14:1, "Pursue love, yet *desire earnestly* spiritual gifts, but especially that you may prophesy" (emphasis mine). The apostle Paul says, by inspiration of the Holy Spirit, "*desire earnestly* spiritual gifts," but some contemporary teachers today say, "do not *desire earnestly* spiritual gifts." It does not take a genius to conclude, correctly, that Paul, under inspiration of the Holy Spirit, knows more about God's will concerning this issue than contemporary teachers. So, by using even simple common sense, one should opt to follow Paul's instructions rather than those who disagree with him. In the same chapter, the apostle Paul says,

> If anyone thinks he is a prophet or spiritual, *let him recognize that the things which I write to you are the Lord's commandment.* But if anyone does not recognize this, *he is not recognized* (emphasis mine, 1 Corinthians 14:37-38).

And, if that is not conclusive enough, Paul finishes by saying,

> Therefore my brethren, *desire earnestly* to prophesy, and *do not forbid to speak in tongues*. But let all things be done properly and in an orderly manner (emphasis mine, 1 Corinthians 14:39-40).

Again, the point is that those who *desire earnestly* and seek the gifts will most likely receive them (Matthew 7:7-11). It is no wonder that the gifts operate far more frequently in Pentecostal churches where they are taught and sought than in non-Pentecostal churches where they are not. What is the "good" that Jesus speaks of in Matthew 7:7-11? Certainly any gift from God is good.

To stay true to the Bible, Christians must not deny that throughout the book of Acts tongues *occasionally* accompanied the infilling with the Holy Spirit. However, to stay true to the Bible, Christians also must not demand that everyone speak in tongues as evidence of a post-salvific infilling with the Holy Spirit. Three thousand people on the day of Pentecost undoubtedly received salvation and the infilling with the Holy Spirit, and yet Luke does not say a single word about them speaking in tongues. *His balance* with regard to reporting the manifestation of tongues *should be our balance* with regard to developing a theology of tongues.

A Post-Conversion Experience

There is one question that has to be answered to the satisfaction of Pentecostals. "If one is filled with (i.e., baptized in) the Holy Spirit upon conversion, then what was it that I experienced post-conversion when I spoke in tongues for the first time?" This is a serious question. I am not denying, as some have done, that people in the Pentecostal ranks are truly speaking in tongues as the Holy Spirit gives them utterance. Speaking in tongues is for today as are all the gifts (though some of them, like that of apostles and prophets, are operating in a limited and lesser sense than in the New Testament). So now Pentecostal Christians must attempt to answer the question, "What was this post-conversion experience that I had?"

Filled Again

As stated above, people are filled, i.e., baptized, with the Holy Spirit at conversion. However, it is curious that on four occasions Luke says that people who were already saved were "filled with the Spirit."

In Acts 4:8 Luke says that Peter was "filled with the Holy Spirit." But Peter was filled with the Holy Spirit in Acts 2. So, then, what is this? It is *another* filling. The passage seems to indicate that Peter was filled anew for a specific purpose. Peter here addresses the "rulers and elders of the people" (v. 8). In fact after the address, Luke says, "Now as they observed the confidence of Peter and John, and understood that they were uneducated and untrained men, they were marveling, and began to recognize them as having been with Jesus" (Acts 4:13). In modern Pentecostal vernacular, Peter was "anointed to preach the word."

In Acts 4:31 Luke says that some who were already Christians were "all filled with the Holy Spirit, and began to speak the word of God with boldness." This is not speaking of the same thing that transpired on the day of Pentecost nor that transpires when one is newly saved and filled with the Holy Spirit. These Christians were filled *again* with the Holy Spirit.

In Acts 7:55 Luke says that Stephen was being filled or "full of the Holy Spirit." But Stephen who was a Christian and obviously already baptized in the Holy Spirit was "full of the Holy Spirit" *again*, and then he faced a martyr's death.

In Acts 13:9 Paul was filled with the Holy Spirit. The apostle Paul was already baptized in the Holy Spirit before this event. Yet, he is spoken of here, in present tense, as "being" filled with the Holy Spirit. When he is filled with the Holy Spirit in this passage, he goes on to pronounce blindness upon Elymas. He was "anointed" to speak judgment upon this "son of the devil" (v. 10).

It is instructive that Luke gives more *explicit* references to people who are already Christians and already baptized in the Holy Spirit receiving a "filling of the Holy Spirit" for what appears to be a *second time* than to people speaking in tongues.

There are *only three* explicit references to people speaking in tongues, but there are *four* explicit references to people who are already Spirit-baptized being *filled with the Spirit*, apparently for the second time. D. A. Carson addresses this issue and says that although he finds no biblical support for a second-blessing theology, he does find support for a second-blessing, a third-blessing, a fourth-blessing, and a fifth-blessing theology.[1] This is precisely my point.

Could it be that my post-conversion experience in which I spoke in tongues was not the first infilling with the Holy Spirit as commonly thought among my brethren, but a second or third experience? Just as in all of the biblical examples when Christians were *again filled* with the Holy Spirit, they did something "under the anointing" of the Holy Spirit, so, likewise, perhaps I was filled with the Holy Spirit to exercise the gift of tongues, the primary gift that I was seeking. What if I had *"desired earnestly to prophesy"* (1 Corinthians 14:39)? Might that have been the gift that would have come forth? Does speaking in tongues happen to be the predominant manifestation of the second (or third, etc.) infilling of the Holy Spirit simply because it is what we Pentecostals are taught to expect?

At this point, one should not be dogmatic about this. However, these questions are on track. It is clear that this is the direction that we Pentecostals should look if we are going to have a more biblical base for our tongues-speaking experiences.

Final Word

Certainly, when one considers Luke's intent and sees the overwhelming references to the filling of the Holy Spirit (soteriological intent) but along with that the obvious lack of references to speaking in tongues (glossolalical intent), one must logically as well as exegetically conclude that Luke is not emphasizing nor attempting to establish a paradigm of tongues as evidence.

Finally, with only three inconsistent references to people speaking in tongues out of twenty-six accounts of Holy Spirit baptisms, we Pentecostal Christians must seriously reconsider our theology that speaking in tongues is the initial, physical evidence of the baptism in the Holy Spirit.

End Notes

[1] D. A. Carson, *Showing the Spirit: A Theological Exposition of 1 Corinthians 12-14* (Grand Rapids, MI.: Baker Book House, 1987), p. 160.

Chapter 15

Study Questions

Study Questions for
Chapter 1
Background Information
---

1. How many years did the author hold to the traditional, Classical Pentecostal position on tongues-as-evidence?

2. What do the words "norm" and "normative" mean in this book (and in theology in general)?

3. Give an example of something that would be a "norm" (or "normative") in the Christian church.

4. Give an example of something that would be normal for Christians but not a "norm" for all Christians.

5. What does the author mean when he says, "While I no

longer believe that speaking in tongues is a 'norm,' I do believe that it is *a normal* Christian experience"?

6. Do Pentecostals as a whole try to allow the Scriptures to establish their creeds and practices?

7. What verse is the "constant refrain" from leader and layman alike in Pentecostal circles?

8. To teach that Pentecostals simply place their experiences above the Scripture is what?

9. The author says that it is not his desire to inflame his Pentecostal colleagues, but it *is* his desire to do what?

Study Questions for
Chapter 2
Do All Speak in Tongues?

---

1. Why does Paul's rhetorical question, "Do all speak in tongues?" not settle the issue of the tongues debate?

2. How complex is the gift of tongues? List some of the variables of operation and function of the gift of tongues.

3. What are the two major categories for speaking in tongues?

4. In which category do Classical Pentecostals believe that *all* Christians *may* speak in tongues?

5. In which category do Classical Pentecostals believe that *all* Christians *shall not* speak in tongues?

6. When a message in tongues is interpreted, the message is equal to what? Give Scripture for support.

Study Questions for Chapter 3
The Initial, Physical Evidence of the Baptism in the Holy Spirit

---

1. When Classical Pentecostals refer to "initial, physical evidence of the baptism in the Holy Spirit," they are referring to what?

2. Briefly, list the five arguments that are advanced in this book.

3. Who or what is the First Wave of the Pentecostal movements?

4. What are the three key things that the First Wave believes?

5. How should the First Wave be subdivided?

6. Can one be a First Wave Pentecostal without being a Classical Pentecostal? Why or why not?

7. Though the author uses the terms *Pentecostal* and *Classical Pentecostal* interchangeably in this work, are these two terms truly synonymous?

8. Who or what is the Second Wave of the Pentecostal movements?

9. What theological distinction separates the Second Wave from the First Wave?

10. Who or what is the Third Wave of the Pentecostal movements?

11. Why does the author say that The United Pentecostal Church should not be lumped together with Classical Pentecostals?

12. For the Classical Pentecostal, what do the words *initial* and *physical* modify? And, why is this significant?

13. Who is it that baptizes people in the Holy Spirit? Give Scripture for support.

14. Are water baptism and Spirit baptism the same thing?

15. Classical Pentecostals argue that there is a difference between receiving the _____ at conversion and receiving the _____ (which for them is subsequent to conversion).

16. Do Classical Pentecostals deny that people receive the "gift of the Holy Spirit" at conversion?

17. What is the "baptism in the Holy Spirit" to Classical Pentecostals?

***Study Questions for
Chapter 4
Setting the Stage***

---

1. Does the author believe or imply that the tongues-as-evidence proponents have missed Luke's soteriological intent?

2. Within the context of the issue of the doctrine of the initial, physical evidence of the baptism in the Holy Spirit, what does the author believe that tongues-as-evidence proponents have done with Lukan soteriology?

3. What is the *Straw Man Fallacy*?

4. What does the author say is Luke's predominant emphasis throughout the book of Acts?

5. How can we prove that the tongues-as-evidence proponents major on the charismatic aspects rather than the salvation aspects within the book of Acts?

6. According to tongues-as-evidence proponent Roger Stronstad, what is devoid of any soteriological connotations?

7. When dealing with the Acts 9 narrative of the gift of the Spirit to Saul (the apostle Paul), what does Stronstad say that Luke's emphasis is not?

8. According to D. W. Kerr, what was Luke emphasizing?

9. Donald A. Johns says that Luke largely ignores both the _____ aspects of the Spirit in the believer and the role of the Spirit in _____.

10. What is it that the tongues-as-evidence proponents emphasize?

11. According to Douglas A. Oss, Luke is careful to emphasize the empowering work of the Spirit rather than the soteriological _____ transformation.

12. What declarative statement in representation of Pentecostals does Oss make?

13. Luke's agenda (intent) as seen by Classical Pentecostals is the Spirit's _____ anointing.

14. Tongues-as-evidence proponents are very clear, and in many cases very adamant, that Luke's emphasis (intent, agenda) throughout the book of Acts is _____.

15. Not only do Classical Pentecostals emphasize the charismatic rather than the soteriological aspects of Luke's writings in Acts, they do so with _____ vigor.

16. Is the author saying that Classical Pentecostals do not see soteriological passages or aspects in the book of Acts?

***Study Questions for
Chapter 5
Argument # 1
Authorial Intent***

---

1. What is the main question to be answered, and the one with which this chapter is most concerned?

2. What is the key to understanding authorial intent?

3. In the face of charges that it is arrogant for one to claim to know the intent of another, how does the author justify searching for Luke's intent?

4. How did Jesus himself make the connection between the "gift my Father promised" and "baptized in the Holy Spirit"?

The Speaking in Tongues Controversy

5. What is the purpose of this promised Holy Spirit? Why is this important in helping to discern Luke's intent?

6. What should those who are frightened to see a *modus operandi* in Acts 2:1-4 do?

7. What does Peter say that one must do to receive the gift of the Holy Spirit?

8. How many on lookers in Acts 2 repented and were baptized in the name of Jesus for the forgiveness of their sins (Acts 2:41)?

9. Even though Luke clearly states that a significant number of people came to faith in Jesus Christ that day, he does not say that they spoke in tongues. Give the two arguments that some Pentecostals have proposed which attempt to explain why Luke does not mention that any of these three thousand spoke in tongues.

10. Does the biblical text say that all three thousand spoke in other tongues as did the 120 in Acts 2:4?

11. Does it appear that Luke is attempting to establish a paradigm about tongues as the initial, physical evidence of the baptism in the Holy Spirit?

12. Why does the author say, "Whether or not the three thousand spoke in tongues does not matter"?

13. If tongues-as-evidence were as important an issue as Classical Pentecostals say it is, what would Luke likely have done with the story of these three thousand converts?

14. What does the author call a "paradigmatic gold mine"?

15. What would have made Luke a very poor communicator?

16. What topic did Luke have no trouble at all communicating about?

17. While tongues should not be elevated above the level given to it in the text of Scripture, neither should tongues be what?

18. To what does the author refer when he speaks of our "biblical right of inference"?

19. With regard to what does the author say that there is no clear statement giving interpreters the right of inference?

20. The number of Holy-Spirit recipients on the first three occasions (in the Acts account) exceeds three thousand people, and yet Luke mentions tongues-speaking with regard to how many people?

21. While one does not have to conclude that tongues is not the initial, physical evidence of the baptism in the Holy Spirit, what should one conclude so far?

22. Thus far, the authorial intent appears to be what?

23. Concerning the account in Acts 8:15-23, Luke does *not* tell us what Simon actually saw. So, how should this affect our dogmatism about this passage?

24. Concerning the account of Saul being filled with the Holy Spirit in Acts 9:17-20, what is the point of Luke's intent? What is he conveying?

25. Is Luke interested in establishing a paradigm for *tongues as the initial, physical evidence* of the baptism

in the Holy Spirit by using Paul as his example?

26. Is Luke interested in establishing a *salvific paradigm* by using Paul as his example?

27. Did Paul ever speak in tongues? Give supporting Scripture.

28. Concerning the account in Acts 10:44-48, what was the first physical evidence that Cornelius (and the other Gentiles present) had received the "gift of the Father" (10:46)?

29. Was Peter convinced that speaking in tongues was the evidence that the Holy Spirit had filled these Gentiles?

30. Why does the author see speaking in tongues in this passage as a soteriological issue?

31. What does the author mean by his statement that "evidence is not the same thing as contingency"?

32. What does the author mean when he says that the manifestation of tongues in the "Cornelius context" is descriptive, not prescriptive?

33. Concerning the account in Acts 19:6, this is only the third account in which people spoke in tongues. However, the text also just as clearly states that they _____.

34. In the three texts, Acts 2, Acts 10, and Acts 19, there is an obvious inconsistency in the *modus operandi* of the outward manifestation of tongues. What does this indicate?

35. Concerning the account in Acts 22:6-16, the apostle

Paul recounts his conversion/baptism in the Holy Spirit experience in exceptional detail. What main point does he leave out?

36. Looking back over all of the accounts of people getting saved and filled with the Holy Spirit, what would you say has been Luke's consistent emphasis (intent)?

***Study Questions for
Chapter 6
Argument # 2
Three Times out of Five?
Does This Establish a Paradigm?***

---

1. Give the syllogism of the the Classical Pentecostal's argument.

2. If Classical Pentecostals are right about the significance of speaking in tongues, then one would expect one of two things in the biblical record. Name both of the two things.

3. The author says that Luke was not trying to teach a theological point about "baptism in the Holy Spirit and speaking in tongues." What then *was* he doing?

4. Since Luke does not make tongues as evidence of the baptism in the Holy Spirit a primary emphasis, how should we view it?

5. In Luke's own record, speaking in tongues is incidental and occasional, not _____ and _____.

6. Why have Classical Pentecostals always thought that

their argument was a deductive one?

7. In Acts 9 (the third occasion—Paul's baptism in the Holy Spirit), does Paul speak in tongues?

8. Does Paul later speak in tongues? Give Scripture for support.

9. Are there only five occurrences in the book of Acts in which people received the baptism in the Holy Spirit?

10. What is the logical fallacy of *begging the question*?

11. How is it that the Classical Pentecostal argument "begs the question"?

12. In Acts 2, three thousand people came to faith in Christ. Whether or not they all spoke in tongues is not the issue. What is the issue?

13. Instead of having three out of five occurrences, there are three out of _____ references to people being saved/baptized in the Holy Spirit throughout the book of Acts.

14. What is the percentage of three out of five? Why is this significant?

15. What is the percentage of three out of twenty-six? Why is this significant?

Study Questions for
Chapter 7
Argument # 3
The Age to Come

1. Gordon Fee says that to be saved is to _____

2. To be filled with the Spirit is to _____

3. When people are not Christians, they are not filled with the Holy Spirit, thus they are not part of _____.

4. The age to come is the description of what?

5. Do Classical Pentecostals deny that Christians who do not speak in tongues have the Holy Spirit in them and the Holy Spirit has initiated them into the age to come?

6. Do Classical Pentecostals deny that non-tongues speakers "have" the Holy Spirit?

7. According to the Classical Pentecostal, what are the "requirements" to be baptized in the Holy Spirit?

8. According to the Classical Pentecostal, what is the evidence that one has been baptized in the Holy Spirit?

9. According to the Bible, what are the "requirements" to be baptized in the Holy Spirit?

10. What is it that the Holy Spirit does for a person at the point of conversion?

11. Is the dual idea that there are Christians who are "spirit-filled" and Christians who are not "spirit-filled" foreign to the New Testament?

12. Classical Pentecostals believe that all Christians "have" the Holy Spirit, just not in "_____."

13. Classical Pentecostals admit that the moment one is converted and accepts Jesus Christ as his Savior, the Holy Spirit immediately _____ in the person, and that person is "a temple of the Holy Spirit" (1 Corinthians 3:16).

14. How did the author's Classical Pentecostal colleague explain the difference between "having the Holy Spirit" and being "baptized in the Holy Spirit"?

15. Gordon Fee says that early Christians did not make what distinction?

16. Why is the phrase "Spirit-filled Christian" an oddity?

17. On the Day of Pentecost, what paradigm was established?

18. Throughout the book of Acts, getting saved included what?

19. Which New Testament writer says, "Seek the baptism in the Holy Spirit"?

Study Questions for
Chapter 8
Argument # 4
The Argument of Subsequence

1. In the three cases (Acts chapters 2, 10, and 19) of people speaking in tongues, was the sequence of events the same?

2. Does Luke make the sequence of events consistent?

3. In the overwhelming majority of conversion experiences throughout the book of Acts, Luke does not what?

4. What does Gordon Fee say concerning the diversity of patterns within the book of Acts?

5. Who has far less to say about sequence than do many Classical Pentecostals?

Study Questions for
Chapter 9
Argument # 5
Historical Narrative Versus Didactic

1. Proper biblical hermeneutics always plays a major part in what?

2. What is one primary hermeneutical principle that is especially germane to this discussion?

3. What is a strong argument that must be considered

when researching the issue of tongues as evidence?

4. Which biblical writer clearly teaches that, "You shall speak in tongues as a result of being baptized in the Holy Spirit"?

5. Shall we simply discard the three accounts in which people spoke in tongues in association with the baptism in the Holy Spirit?

6. Should we elevate to a theological dogma the three accounts in which people spoke in tongues?

7. What truth can be gleaned from the historical narrative that Luke supplies?

8. What does not follow from the historical narrative that Luke supplies?

Study Questions for
Chapter 10
History: Not on the Side of Evidence

---

1. Has speaking in tongues been absent from the church throughout the last 2,000 years?

2. The author says, there is one aspect concerning the tongues issue that is absent from church history. What is it?

3. Throughout the history of the church there was no connection between the baptism in the _____ Spirit and speaking in _____.

4. When did the the tongues-as-evidence doctrine begin,

and who originated and popularized it?

5. Do you think that it is significant that the tongues-as-evidence argument enjoys no representation in the overall history of the church until only recently?

Study Questions for
Chapter 11
Why Tongues?

---

1. Where does the Bible say (or even imply) that tongues-speaking is to be used to preach the gospel to other peoples?

2. Stanley Horton says that the various tongues emphasized God's promise to do what?

3. Why doesn't Luke say that all or even some of the other three thousand who were saved on the day of Pentecost spoke in tongues?

4. What was one reason that the Gentiles in Acts 10 spoke in tongues?

5. Are the few occurrences in the Bible of tongues-speaking enough to establish a paradigm for all to have to follow?

Study Questions for Chapter 12
Are Tongues the Least?

1. Where does Paul say, "The gift of tongues is the least of the gifts"?

2. Is the gift of tongues consistently listed last in the various lists of gifts?

3. Why does the author say that "an overemphasis upon a sheer itemization would undoubtedly be gratuitous"?

4. Which gift is listed last in 1 Corinthians 12:8-10 and 1 Corinthians 12:29-30?

5. Which fruit of the Spirit in Galatians 5:22-23 is listed last?

6. Of the items listed in 1 Corinthians 13:13, is the least one listed last?

7. Concerning the best gifts, what is the context in which Paul says that prophecy is greater than tongues?

8. Did Paul speak in tongues very much?

9. Was Paul thankful that he spoke in tongues? If so, to whom did he direct his gratitude?

10. When Paul said "He who speaks in a tongue edifies himself," was this a condemnation of speaking in tongues?

11. Is it wrong to edify oneself?

12. What would show Paul as having a glaring double standard?

13. Is Paul contrasting tongues and prophecy as "bad and good"?

14. Which gifts are the best gifts, and why?

***Study Questions for
Chapter 13
Evidence or Accompaniment?***

---

1. Why is the term "evidence" with regard to tongues and the baptism in the Holy Spirit misleading?

2. What was tongues an evidence of in Acts 2?

3. What was tongues an evidence of in Acts 10?

4. What was tongues an evidence of in Acts 19?

5. How many passages of Scripture in the book of Acts explicitly mention speaking in tongues?

6. When we jump from the early disciples' Holy-Spirit-infilling experiences set solidly in a soteriological context to our post-salvific, subsequent infilling, what do we miss?

7. Where in Acts or in any other New Testament book is the "baptism in the Holy Spirit" spoken of and promoted in the fashion as is done by Classical Pentecostals today?

8. The author believes that it is far more accurate to

simply see speaking in tongues as an occasional _____ of the infilling of the Holy Spirit.

***Study Questions for
Chapter 14
A Recapitulation and Concluding Remarks***

---

1. The author concludes that it is quite obvious that Luke's overall intent was soteriological and not glossolalical. Do you agree or disagree? Why?

2. The author argues that the Classical Pentecostal paradigm of "Three Times out of Five" is false. He argues that it is really three out of twenty-six occurrences. Do you agree or disagree? Why?

3. Gordon Fee says that to be saved *is to be filled with the Spirit*. Do you agree or disagree? Why?

4. The author argues that there is no normative sequence of events derived from Acts 2, Acts 10, and Acts 19. Do you agree or disagree? Why?

5. The author argues that Christians should be very careful when building their doctrines upon narrative portions of Scripture. Do you agree or disagree? Why?

6. The author implies that a lack of history is an important fact in the tongues-as-evidence argument. Do you agree or disagree? Why?

7. The author argues that there are two extremes with regard to tongues, and both are wrong. One extreme is that speaking in tongues is not for today. The other extreme is that tongues were and always are the

initial, physical evidence of the baptism in the Holy Spirit. Do you agree or disagree that both of these positions are extremes? Why?

8. The author points out that in 1 Corinthians 14:1, Paul *encourages* Christians to seek the gifts. Do you agree or disagree? Why?

9. The author says that to stay true to the Bible, Christians must not deny that throughout the book of Acts tongues *occasionally* accompanied the infilling with the Holy Spirit. Do you agree or disagree? Why?

10. The author also says that to stay true to the Bible, Christians must not demand that everyone speak in tongues as evidence of the infilling with the Holy Spirit. Do you agree or disagree? Why?

11. The author says that Luke's *balance* with regard to reporting the manifestation of tongues *should be our balance* with regard to developing a theology of tongues. Do you agree or disagree? Why?

12. In answering the question of many Pentecostals, "What was this post-conversion experience that I had?" the author says that it is likely *another* filling—a new filling for a specific purpose. Do you agree or disagree? Why?

13. The author argues that Luke was not emphasizing nor attempting to establish a paradigm of tongues as evidence. Do you agree or disagree? Why?

Bibliography

Barclay, William. <u>The Promise of the Spirit</u>. Philadelphia, PA.: The Westminster Press, 1976.

Barrett, C. K. <u>The First Epistle To The Corinthians</u>. New York: Harper & Row, Publishers, 1968.

Bennett, Dennis, and Rita. <u>The Holy Spirit and You</u>. Plainfield, N.J.: Logos International, 1971.

Bicket, Zenas J. <u>We Hold These Truths</u>. Springfield, MO.: Gospel Publishing House, 1978.

Bittlinger, Arnold. <u>Gifts and Graces</u>. Grand Rapids, MI.: Wm. B. Eerdmans Publishing Co., 1967.

_____ . <u>Gifts and Ministries</u>. Grand Rapids, MI.: Wm. B. Eerdmans Publishing Co., 1973.

Blaiklock, E. M. <u>The Acts of the Apostles</u>. Tyndale New Testament Commentaries, gen, ed. R. V. G. Tasker, no. 5. Grand Rapids, MI.: Wm. B. Eerdmans Publishing Co., 1977.

Bridge, Donald and Phypers, David. Spiritual Gifts and the Church. Downers Grove, IL.: Inter-Varsity Press, 1973.

Bruce, F. F. The Book of Acts. The New International Commentary on the New Testament, gen. ed. F. F. Bruce. Grand Rapids, MI.: Wm. B. Eerdmans Publishing Co., 1977.

Brumback, Carl. What Meaneth This? Springfield, MO.: Gospel Publishing House, 1947.

Burns, Lanier J. "A Reemphasis on the Purpose of the Sign Gifts." Bibliotheca Sacra 132, no. 527 (July-September 1975): 242-249.

Carlson, G. Raymond. "Christ's Gifts to His Church." Pentecostal Evangel, 29 July 1990, 4-6.

_____. "The Role of the Prophet Today." Pentecostal Evangel, 5 August 1990, 4-5.

Carson, D. A. From Triumphalism to Maturity. Grand Rapids, MI.: Baker Book House, 1984.

_____. Exegetical Fallacies. Grand Rapids, MI.: Baker Book House, 1984.

_____. Showing the Spirit. Grand Rapids, MI.: Baker Book House, 1987.

Dresselhaus, Richard L. "The Interpretation of Tongues" Paraclete 6 no. 4, (1972): 7-12.

Ervin, Howard M. These are not Drunken as Ye Suppose. Plainfield, N.J.: Logos International, 1968.

Fee, Gordon D. The First Epistle to the Corinthians. The

New International Commentary on the New Testament, gen. ed. F. F. Bruce. Grand Rapids, MI.: Wm. B. Eerdmans Publishing Co., 1988.

_____. Gospel and Spirit: Issues in New Testament Hermeneutics. Peabody, MA.: Hendrickson Publishers, Inc., 1991.

_____. "Response to Roger Stronstad's 'The Biblical Precedent for Historical Precedent'" Paraclete 27, no. 3 (1993): pp. 11-14.

_____. God's Empowering Presence: The Holy Spirit in the Letters of Paul. Peabody: Hendrickson Publishers, Inc., 1994.

_____. Paul, the Spirit, and the People of God. Peabody: Hendrickson Publishers, Inc., 1996.

Flyn, Leslie B. Nineteen Gifts of the Spirit. Wheaton, IL.: Victor Books, 1974.

Gangel, Kenneth O. You and Your Spiritual Gifts. Chicago, IL.: Moody Press, 1975.

_____. Unwrap Your Spiritual Gifts. Wheaton, IL.: Victor Books, 1988.

Gee, Donald. Concerning Spiritual Gifts. Springfield, MO.: Gospel Publishing House, 1972.

_____. Now That You've Been Baptized in the Spirit. Springfield, MO.: Gospel Publishing House, 1972.

_____. "Spiritual Gifts." Paraclete 1, no. 1 (Fall 1967): 23-26.

_____. Spiritual Gifts in the Work of the Ministry

<u>Today</u>. Springfield, MO.: Gospel Publishing House, 1963.

Gentile, Ernest B. <u>Your Sons & Daughters Shall Prophesy: Prophetic Gifts in Ministry Today</u>. Grand Rapids, MI.: Chosen Books, 1999.

Godet, F. <u>Commentary on St. Paul's First Epistle to the Corinthians</u>. Vol 2. English translation from the French by A. Cusin, Edinburgh, 1886; repr. Grand Rapids, MI., 1957.

Grossman, Sigfried. <u>There are Other Gifts than Tongues</u>. Wheaton, IL.: Tyndale House Publishers, 1973.

Grudem, Wayne, gen. ed. <u>Are Miraculous Gifts for Today? Four Views</u> (Cessationist, Gaffen, Richard B. Jr.), (Open but Cautious, Saucy, Robert L.), (Third Wave, Storms, C. Samuel), (Pentecostal/Charismatic, Oss, Douglas A). Grand Rapids: Zondervan Publishing House, 1996.

Hadden, Andrew G. "Gifts of the Spirit in Assemblies of God Writings." <u>Paraclete</u> 24, no. 1 (Winter 1990): 20-32.

Harrington, Hanna K., and Patten, Rebecca. "Pentecostal Hermeneutics and Postmodern Literary Theory." <u>Pneuma</u>, 16, no. 1, (Spring 1994): 109-114.

Ho, Melvin. "A Comparison of Glossolalia in Acts and Corinthians." <u>Paraclete</u> 20, no. 2 (Spring 1986): 15-19.

Holdcroft, Thomas L. <u>The Holy Spirit</u>. Springfield, MO.: Gospel Publishing House, 1979.

_____. "Spirit Baptism: Its Nature and Chronology."

Paraclete 1, no. 1 (Fall 1967): 27-30.

Horton, Harold. The Gifts of the Spirit. Springfield, MO.: Gospel Publishing House, 1975.

Horton, Stanley M. What The Bible Says About The Holy Spirit. Springfield, MO.: Gospel Publishing House, 1976.

_____. The Radiant Commentary on the New Testament. Springfield, MO.: Gospel Publishing House, 1981. The Book of Acts.

_____. ed. Systematic Theology A Pentecostal Perspective. Springfield, MO.: Gospel Publishing House, 1994.

Jeter, Hugh P. "Praying for Signs and Wonders." Pentecostal Evangel, 5 November 1989, 6-7.

Kinghorn, Kenneth Cain. Gifts of the Spirit. Nashville, TN.: Abingdon Press, 1976.

Kinnaman, Gary D. And Signs Shall Follow. Grand Rapids, MI.: Revell, 1988.

Levang, Raymond K. "The Content of an Utterance in Tongues." Paraclete 23, no 1 (1989): 14-20.

Lim, David. Spiritual Gifts: A Fresh Look. Springfield, MO.: Gospel Publishing House, 1991.

MacGorman, Jack W. The Gifts of the Spirit. Nashville, TN.: Broadman Press, 1974.

McGee, Gary B. Initial Evidence. Peabody, MA.: Hendrickson Publishing, 1991.

McRae, William J. The Dynamics of Spiritual Gifts. Grand Rapids, MI.: Zondervan Publishing Co., 1976.

Morris, Leon. The First Epistle of Paul to the Corinthians. Tyndale New Testament Commentaries, gen. ed. R. V. G. Tasker, no. 7. Grand Rapids, MI.: Wm. B. Eerdmans Publishing Co., 1981.

Munyon, Tim. "Transitional Sign or Continued Practice?" Paraclete 21, no. 2 (Spring 1987): 18-20.

_____. "The Gift of Prophecy—Its Regulation and Purpose." Paraclete 4, no. 4 (Fall 1970): 7-12.

Palma, Anthony D. "The Gift of Prophecy—It's Nature and Scope." Paraclete, 4, no. 3 (1970): 8-13.

Pytches, David. Spiritual Gifts in the Local Church. Minneapolis, MN.: Bethany House Publishers, 1985.

Riggs, Ralph M. The Spirit Himself. Springfield, MO.: Gospel Publishing House, 1949.

Smalley, Stephen S. "Spiritual Gifts and 1 Corinthians 12-16." Journal of Biblical Literature 87, 4 (December 1968): 427-433.

Stronstad, Roger. "The Biblical Precedent for Historical Precedent" Paraclete, vol. 27, no. 3 (1993): pp. 1-10.

_____. "Trends in Pentecostal Hermeneutics." Paraclete 22, no. 3 (Summer 1988): 1-12.

_____. *The Charismatic Theology of St. Luke.* Peabody, MA.: Hendrickson Publishers, Inc., 1984.

Thee, Francis C. R. "Wherefore Tongues." Paraclete 3, no. 1 (1969): 14-20.

Torrey, R. A. <u>The Baptism with the Holy Spirit</u>. Minneapolis, MN.: Bethany House Publishers, 1972.

Wagner, C. Peter. <u>Your Spiritual Gifts Can Help Your Church Grow</u>. Ventura, CA.: Regal Books, 1979.

_____. ed. <u>Signs and Wonders Today</u>. Altamonte Springs, FL.: Creation House Strang Communications Company, 1987.

Williams, Rodman J. <u>Renewal Theology</u>. Grand Rapids, MI.: Zondervan Publishing Co., 1990.

Wimber, John. <u>A Brief Sketch of Signs and Wonders Through the Church Age</u>. Placentia, CA.: Vineyard Christian Fellowship.

Glossary

Age to come: A description that the Bible uses for that future time when all things shall be under Christ's reign.

Apologetics (apologists): The defense of the faith (those who defend the faith).

Baptism in the Holy Spirit: The event in which the Holy Spirit takes up residency in a believer. Some think that this happens at conversion while others believe that it is subsequent to conversion and is accompanied by the evidence of speaking in tongues.

Begging the question: An argument where the conclusion is "embedded" in the premise. Sometimes called a circular argument because the conclusion becomes the premise.

Cessationism: The belief that the outward and more demonstrative gifts have ceased.

Contingency: Something dependent on the conditions or occurrences of something else.

Deductive (deduction): The drawing of a conclusion through reasoning; a conclusion that follows necessarily from the stated premises.

Descriptive: A statement or an account describing how something was or is.

Dogma (theological): An authoritative belief or statement of beliefs considered to be absolutely true.

Dogmatic (dogmatism): Characterized by an authoritative, emphatic stance.

Edify: To encourage in intellectual, moral, or spiritual improvement.

Eisegesis: Reading meaning of one's own opinions or ideas into the text.

Exegesis (exegetes): Drawing meaning out of the text, rather than eisegesis, which is reading your own meaning into the text. An exegete is a person who does exegesis.

Glossolalia: Speaking in tongues.

Glossolalical: Related to speaking in tongues.

Hermeneutics: The art and science of biblical interpretation.

Historical narrative: Accounts in the Bible that describe stories and events that are of a historical nature.

Infer: To conclude from evidence or premises.

Imply: To express or indicate indirectly.

Norm (normative): Something that is binding upon all Christians; a "must" or a "have to."

Normal: Something that may but does not have to happen in a Christian's life. If it does, that's okay. And if it doesn't, that's okay too.

Lukan: Luke's writings or intent.

Manifestation: An outward appearing of something; typically the gifts are said to be manifestations of the Holy Spirit.

Modus operandi: A method of operation.

Paradigm (also paradigmatic): An example that serves as pattern or model.

Pneumatology: Of or relating to the Holy Spirit.

Pneumatological: Something relating to the Holy Spirit in

a charismatic sense.

Prescriptive: Giving injunctions, directions, laws, or rules about how something should (or must) be done.

Prose: Ordinary speech or writing, without metrical structure.

Right of inference: The biblical right—because of other clear passages of Scripture—to infer, or draw a certain conclusion.

Salvific: Having to do with salvation.

Soteriological: Having to do with salvation.

Subsequence: Following in time or order; succeeding.

Syllogism: A form of deductive reasoning consisting of a major premise, a minor premise, and a conclusion.

Xenoglossa: Real languages.

Xenoglossolalia: Speaking in real languages.

About the Author

Rick Walston is founder and president of Columbia Evangelical Seminary in Washington state where he serves as a professor of theology. He is also an adjunct professor with Potchefstroom University.

Before going into full time academics, he pastored for two decades in both Assemblies of God churches and independent churches.

Dr. Walston's educational background is eclectic and extensive. It includes a D.Min. in pastoral studies from the Northwest Graduate School of the Ministry, and a Ph.D. in New Testament Theology from Potchefstroom University.

He is the author of several books, including:

Unraveling the Mystery of the Motivational Gifts: Your Gifts Discovery Manual (Xulon Press, 2002)

Walston's Guide to Christian Distance Learning: Earning Degrees Nontraditionally, 4th edition (Persuasion Press, 1999)

Divorce and Remarriage: An Amplification of the Assemblies of God Position Paper on Divorce and Remarriage (Gospel Publishing House, 1991)

Visit the Columbia Evangelical Seminary web site at: www.ColumbiaSeminary.edu

Dr. Walston can be reached via email at: CES@tx3.net

Or by regular mail at: *Columbia Evangelical Seminary*
P. O. Box 1189
Buckley, WA 98321

www.ingramcontent.com/pod-product-compliance
Lightning Source LLC
Chambersburg PA
CBHW070312230426
43663CB00011B/2105